GW00359862

...101?

101 Wines searched high and low to find the finest wines in Ireland. It couldn't have been easier - all of them, and many more, were just Next Door. With over 50 locations nationwide, and with the widest selection of old and new world wines, we are your first stop for the best wine in the country.

To find your nearest Next Door Wines please log on to www.nextdoor.ie

NEXT DOOR
HOME OF GOOD WINE

Enjoy Alcohol Sensibly
Visit drinkaware.ie

For Information about EuroCave
email: eurocave@febvre.ie
or call: 01 216 1400
www.eurocave.com

EuroCave®

If you're passionate about wine

101 Great Wines under €12

Mary Dowey

A. & A. Farmar

© Mary Dowey 2008

All rights reserved. No part of this publication may be reproduced in any form or by any means without the prior permission of the publisher or else under the terms of a licence permitting photocopying issued by the Irish Copyright Licensing Agency or a similar reproductive rights organisation.

British Library Cataloguing in Publication Data
A CIP catalogue record for this book is available from
the British Library

ISBN 978-1-906353-06-3

Published by
A. & A. Farmar Ltd
78 Ranelagh Village, Dublin 6
Ireland
Tel (01) 496 3625
afarmar@iol.ie
www.aafarmar.ie

Cover design by Kevin Gurry
Typesetting by Bookworks
Printed and bound by GraphyCems

Contents

Introduction

This small book is one of the most rewarding projects I have worked on in thirteen years of wine writing. Why? Simply because it has been so exciting to find a vast array of cracking wines on sale in Ireland at less than €12. It would have been easier to choose 202 of them than 101! But, after several months of rigorous tasting and ruthless pruning, I have ended up with a final selection of great bottles—wines that I would be delighted to see on a dinner table any time. In addition to these super buys, I have picked out ten terrific sparkling wines costing less than €15.

Both as a wine writer and as a consumer, I have always championed wines of decent quality at everyday prices. I get more of a kick out of discovering a new supermarket gem at €9.99 and putting it to the test with an omelette on a Tuesday night than sampling a thimbleful of an indecently expensive Bordeaux *cru classé* at a swish tasting. Now, as we face into difficult times economically, the realisation that it is possible to enjoy an endless variety of great wines without spending a fortune is more cheering than ever.

Tastes and trends

Wine likes and dislikes are, to a large extent, personal—so inevitably my own tastes have influenced the selection of wines. But current trends are also strongly reflected in the line-up—see *5 Key Trends in Wine Today*, page xi.

Star wines

It is often said that the better a wine tastes, the more difficult it is to describe. The appeal is powerful and immediate – the liquid equivalent of love at first sight or what the French describe as a *coup de coeur*. The wines marked with a star all fall into this category. They seem to me to offer something extra-special. Try them and see whether you experience that same sense of supercharged attraction!

The kitchen table test

I am passionately opposed to over-hasty judgements about wine—so no wines are recommended on the basis of a quick mouthful at a tasting event. All were sampled slowly at my kitchen table. Many I then re-tasted with food.

Matching food and wine

Even the cheapest wine and the simplest snack can taste sensational together if their flavours harmonise— so it's worth having a good look at the food suggestions for each wine.

Easy availability

All of the recommended wines are available either by mail order via the internet or in leading supermarkets and/or independent off-licences.

Prices

The price quoted for each wine is almost invariably that supplied to me by the importer as the recommended retail price at the time of going to press. But as retailers are free to charge what they like, prices may vary substantially from one outlet to another, possibly climbing above €12 in certain shops.

In a few instances, a recommended wine costs less than €12 only in the specific outlet mentioned; it may well be available in many other shops but at a higher price.

As far as internet sales are concerned, please note that the bottle price quoted may only apply when a minimum quantity of wine is ordered, and delivery may cost extra.

Strike out!

To me, the most depressing wine drinker is the one who says: 'I know what I like and I stick to it.' There are so many terrific wine styles to try—made from heaps of different grapes in heaps of different countries. Strike out! You have 101 reasons to be adventurous.

Mary Dowey

Europe fights back

The New World wine-producing countries have steadily increased their market share in Ireland in recent years while Europe's wine producers have lost ground. But now France, Italy and Spain are fighting back—particularly at the less expensive end of the market.

One of my biggest surprises, while working on this book, was to discover the wealth of well-made, individualistic and inexpensive wines currently on offer from Europe—particularly from France and Spain. The greatest disappointment was to find relatively few exciting under-€12 wines from Australia—the country with the biggest slice of the Irish market, and one which I enormously admire. These days Australia seems to perform much more impressively in the €12–€17 zone.

Why low prices can equal bad value

Most of the wines in this book sell at €9–€12, not less. Why? Because the fixed costs associated with a bottle of wine are so high that most really cheap wines tend to be of dismal quality. Excise duty alone eats up €2.05 of the retail price, which must also include 21% VAT and cover wholesale and retail margins besides contributing to packaging, transport and warehousing overheads. In a bottle at €5.99, the value of the actual wine is only about 50 cent. In a bottle at €9.99, the wine is worth €2.22—over four times as much (even though the retail price is less than double). So it makes sense to trade up. Drinkable €5.99 miracles are rare.

5 key trends in wine today

Lower alcohol

Big, headsplitting blockbusters are on the way out. Light, zesty whites like Riesling and Sauvignon Blanc are in, in, in.

Rosé on a roll

Pink wines are super-trendy—but we shouldn't wait for the sun. Most rosés are terrific with spicy foods, all year round.

Green wines

More and more wines are being produced by eco-friendly methods—even if they aren't necessarily certified as organic.

The bubbles boom

Sparkling wines of all kinds are in higher demand than ever. If it can't be champagne it can be prosecco, cava or New World fizz.

The Syrah/Shiraz show

The world's most fashionable red grape variety. Easier to drink than Cabernet, funkier than Merlot.

Screwcaps—a turn for the better

Screwcaps are indicated throughout the text because I strongly support them. For one thing, they avoid the risk of cork taint—the process whereby a bacterial compound, sometimes present in cork, spoils a wine's flavours. Currently this musty-smelling mould is responsible for adversely affecting the taste of up to 5 per cent of cork-sealed wines. (Dozens of bottles of corked wine were poured down my sink during 101 tasting sessions.)

A further bonus is that wines bottled under screwcap keep fresher for longer—a fact which emerged vividly on my latest trip to Australia. Visiting various producers and sampling their wines back through many years, I found it easy to tell by smell alone at which point screwcaps had been introduced. The wines bottled under cork smelt staler, much less vibrant.

So, the next time you see a screwcapped bottle, smile and be grateful!

The year on the bottle—does it matter?

When you are buying inexpensive wines, it's not worth worrying whether the vintage on the bottle was a particularly good one or not. Instead, think about the age of the wine. Most light, crisp white wines and rosés should be drunk as young as possible (i.e. within a year or so of the vintage). Medium-bodied whites and reds can be a little older (2–3 years), and richer reds a bit older still (3–4 years). Beware of dodgy antiques.

5 fast ways to increase your wine fun

Buy decent glasses
Of clear, thin glass, coming in at the top like a tulip. Fill them only as far as the widest point—see why below.

Swirl, sniff and ponder
Half the pleasure of wine comes from sniffing the aromas. But you can't swirl the glass to release them if it's too full!

Don't overchill whites or overheat reds
Very cold white wines have precious little flavour. Warmed red wines often taste syrupy and flat.

Play at food matching
Some food and wine flavours taste fabulous together. Others clash. Experiment and make up your own mind.

Pay a few euro more
Better quality is not absolutely guaranteed, but it's likely. See 'Why low prices can equal poor value', page x.

Find a few names you trust—and remember them

How many times have you thoroughly enjoyed a wine. . . without having the faintest clue what it was called a few days later? There's no point saying 'it was a Rioja' or 'it was a white Burgundy' because, in quality terms, the name of a wine region means absolutely nothing. Almost the reverse, in fact: some of the poshest regions are also the most profiteering, pumping out oceans of dire plonk.

The only reliable pointer to quality is the producer's name or the brand name. So, any time you like a wine, try to remember that. You can then try other wines from the same producer with a reasonable hope of success. Every so often, add a new name to your list of likes. A small wine notebook in the kitchen will ease the mental struggle.

LIGHT AND REFRESHING WHITES

Alain Brumont Gros Manseng-Sauvignon Blanc Vin de Pays des Côtes de Gascogne

Gascony, South-West France
€11.35

Vintage: 2007
Grape: Gros Manseng, Sauvignon Blanc
Alcohol: 12.5%
Plus point: Among 10 Bottles Most Likely to Impress a Wine Buff, page 118
Food matches: Aperitif; salads (including smoked salmon salad); light, spicy dishes; goat's cheese tart

No wonder Brumont is a big name in south-west France. This is like Sauvignon Blanc with three times the usual intensity of fruity charm and a tiny but exotic hint of spice, thanks to the Basque grape Gros Manseng. An aromatic treat.

Stockists: *Mail order* *www.lecaveau.ie*
Kilkenny *Le Caveau, Kilkenny; and other independent stockists*

Alpha Zeta 'P' Pinot Grigio delle Venezie

Veneto, North-East Italy
€11.99

Vintage: 2007
Grape: Pinot Grigio
Alcohol: 12.5%
Plus point: Screwcap
Food matches: Aperitif; mixed antipasti; light fish dishes; seafood, vegetable or lemon risottos; pasta in a lemon/cream sauce

Pinot Grigio is so often wishy-washy that it's a pleasure to come across one with enough personality to stand far out from the crowd. This is super-smooth and flavoursome, leaving a refreshing trail of lemon behind as it slips down.

Stockists: *Mail order* wineonline.ie
Cork O'Donovans outlets **Dublin** Bin No. 9, Goatstown; Donnybrook Fair, Donnybrook; Drink Store, Manor St; Enowine, IFSC & Monkstown; Fallon & Byrne, Exchequer St; Hole in the Wall, Blackhorse Ave; Lilac Wines, Fairview; Malt House, James St; Red Island, Skerries **Kilkenny** Le Caveau, Kilkenny

Chablis Thomas de Ribens

Northern Burgundy, France
€8.99

Vintage: 2007
Grape: Chardonnay
Alcohol: 12.5%
Food matches: Aperitif; fish and seafood of all kinds—salmon and oysters especially

Purists may argue that this wine from Ireland's favourite Burgundy region is a tad dilute. Too bad. It has charm and drinkability on its side, offering classic Chablis flavours—ripe apples, lemon, honey and a fresh, mineral tang—at a remarkably low price.

Stockists: *Almost nationwide Lidl*

Château de la Bretesche Muscadet Sèvre et Maine Sur Lie

Western Loire Valley, France
€9.99

Vintage: 2006/7
Grape: Melon de Bourgogne
Alcohol: 12%
Food matches: Aperitif; salads; seafood (especially oysters and mussels); light fish dishes

If more wines from this once-adored region were as good as this one, Muscadet would come galloping into fashion. It's mouthwateringly crisp but not austere, with delicious, honey-tinged apple notes—but don't overchill it or you'll miss them.

Stockists: *Almost nationwide* O'Briens

Château des Eyssards Bergerac Sec

Bergerac, South-West France
€9.80

Vintage: 2007
Grape: Sauvignon Blanc, Sémillon
Alcohol: 13.5%
Plus point: Among 10 Best Wines for a Posh Dinner, page 49
Food matches: Aperitif; many light foods—salads; fish or seafood; chicken; dishes based on green vegetables or goat's cheese

One of two terrific Bergeracs in this book. (The other is on the next page.) Aromas of ripe Cox's apples and passion fruit will draw you in—and keep you hooked as they mutate into a feast of intense, citrus-edged flavours.

Stockists: *Mail order* www.winesdirect.ie

Château Pique-Sègue Montravel ★

Bergerac, South-West France
€9.99

Vintage: 2007
Grape: Sauvignon Blanc, Sémillon, Muscadelle
Alcohol: 12%
Plus point: Among 10 Best Wines for a Big Party, page 66
Food matches: Aperitif; many light foods—salads; fish or seafood;
chicken; dishes based on green vegetables or goat's cheese

I simply don't understand how a wine with so much style and appeal can sell at such a dazzling price. Layers of zesty flavour come wrapped in a satin texture and unfold slowly, lingering deliciously in a long, lime-fresh finish.

Stockists: *Dublin Bin No 9, Goatstown; Boomers, Clondalkin; Coach House, Ballinteer; Comet, Santry; Donnybrook Fair; Eurospar, Rathcoole; Gibneys, Malahide; Goose, Drumcondra; Jus de Vine, Portmarnock; Molloys outlets; O'Neills, SC Rd; Orchard, Applewood; Redmonds, Ranelagh; Vintry, Rathgar* **Galway** *Vineyard, Galway* **Kildare** *Mill Wine Cellar, Maynooth* **Meath** *Bunch of Grapes, Clonee; Next Door, Enfield* **Roscommon** *Dalys, Boyle* **Tipperary** *Lonergans, Clonmel* **Waterford** *Ardkeen Stores, Waterford* **Wicklow** *Wicklow Arms, Delgany*

Cusumano Insolia Sicilia

Sicily, Italy
€11.99

Vintage: 2007
Grape: Insolia
Alcohol: 13%
Food matches: Aperitif; salads; fish with a squeeze of lemon or fish pie; light pasta dishes; vegetable or seafood pizzas; cold chicken

If you're weary of familiar white grape varieties like Chardonnay and Sauvignon Blanc, try this Sicilian speciality and relish the difference. Round and delicately peachy, it delivers lovely lemon freshness all the way through.

Stockists: *Dublin* *Bennetts, Howth; Bin No. 9, Goatstown; Cellars Big Wine Warehouse, Naas Rd; Donnybrook Fair, Donnybrook; Jus de Vine, Portmarnock; Kielys, Mount Merrion; Lilac Wines, Fairview; McCabes, Blackrock & Foxrock; McHughs, Artane & Kilbarrack **Galway** Harvest outlets **Laois** Egans, Portlaoise **Louth** Callans, Dundalk **Offaly** Lynchs Bottleshop, Tullamore **Tipperary** Eldons, Clonmel; Lonergans, Clonmel **Waterford** Ardkeen Stores, Waterford; Worldwide Wines, Waterford **Wexford** Greenacres, Wexford **Wicklow** Hollands, Bray*

Devil's Corner Sauvignon Blanc

Tasmania, Australia
€11.99

Vintage: 2007
Grape: Sauvignon Blanc
Alcohol: 13%
Plus point: Screwcap; among 10 Best Wines for a Posh Dinner, page 49
Food matches: Aperitif; salads; delicate fish or seafood (with or without an Asian twist); Thai green curries; asparagus dishes; guacamole

From cool Tasmania, here comes a grapefruity Sauvignon Blanc which gives many pricier rivals from New Zealand a serious run for their money. Pure pleasure, with a grassy edge and hint of minerality for extra interest.

Stockists: *Cork O'Donovans outlets **Dublin** Coach House, Ballinteer; Goose, Drumcondra; Jus de Vine, Portmarnock; McCabes, Blackrock & Foxrock; McHughs, Artane & Kilbarrack; Redmonds, Ranelagh **Galway** Salthill Liquor Store, Salthill **Sligo** Currids, Sligo **Tipperary** Kellers Take Home, Roscrea; Lonergans, Clonmel **Waterford** Worldwide Wines, Waterford **Wicklow** Capranis, Ashford; Hollands, Bray*

Dourthe No 1 Bordeaux Sauvignon Blanc

Bordeaux, France
€11.49

Vintage: 2007
Grape: Sauvignon Blanc
Alcohol: 12%
Plus point: Screwcap
Food matches: Aperitif; salads; fish; seafood; egg or vegetable dishes (especially with mint or other herbs)

This classy effort offers more depth of flavour than many examples of Sauvignon Blanc at a similar price. Although juicy and bracing with attractive herbal notes, it tastes of beautifully ripe grapes. Not something Bordeaux can always achieve!

Stockists: *Almost nationwide O'Briens*

www.approachwines.com

Dedication, passion,
expertise, local knowledge –
an unrivalled combination

Approach Trade

Flying Kiwi Marlborough Sauvignon Blanc

Marlborough, New Zealand
€9.99

Vintage: 2007
Grape: Sauvignon Blanc
Alcohol: 12.5%
Plus point: Screwcap; among 10 Best Wines for a Big Party, page 66; also 10 Best Wines for Christmas, page 133; 1% of revenue goes to kiwi conservation
Food matches: Aperitif; salads; fish; seafood (especially spicy crab cakes); pasta with pesto; Thai green curries

So skilfully has New Zealand's Marlborough region carved out a starry reputation for Sauvignon Blanc that there's precious little of it to be had for under €12—let alone under €10. Aromatic, lively and absolutely typical, this is a minor miracle.

Stockists: *Almost nationwide* Eurospar; Mace; Spar

Gavi La Battistina

Piedmont, North-West Italy
€9.99

Vintage: 2007
Grape: Cortese
Alcohol: 12%
Food matches: Aperitif; delicate fish or shellfish; lemon, green vegetable or seafood risottos

This terrific wine delivers a zesty burst of citrus cushioned in softer flavours of pears and white peaches, yet the finish is bone-dry. Mouthwatering down to the last drop: I know—I finished the bottle. From posh (expensive) Gavi, a real bargain.

Stockists: *Almost nationwide* O'Briens

10 best recession-busters

Aperitif

- Marks & Spencer Dry Fino Sherry
  €7.49 (page 127)

White

- Kiwi Cuvée Sauvignon Blanc, Vin de Pays du Val de Loire
  €6.99 (page 15)
- Inycon Fiano Sicilia
  €7.99 (page 14)
- Tramoya Verdejo Rueda
  €7.99 (page 29)

Rosé

- Chivite Gran Feudo Navarra Rosado
  €8.99–€9.99 (page 50)

Red

- Tesco Argentina Malbec Reserve
  €5.99 (page 119)
- Altano Douro
  €8.99 (page 79)
- Corinto Merlot
  €8.95 (page 65)
- Geoff Merrill Cabernet-Merlot
  €8.99 (page 100)
- The Wolftrap Syrah-Mourvèdre-Viognier
  €8.99 (page 122)

Inycon Estate Fiano Sicilia

Sicily, Italy
€7.99

Vintage: 2007
Grape: Fiano
Alcohol: 13%
Plus point: Screwcap; among 10 Best Recession-Busters, page 13
Food matches: Aperitif; light salads; fish (including fish and chips); shellfish; pasta with pesto or lemon/cream sauce

Although it still wafts out familiar, subtle aromas of peaches and fresh lemon juice, this version of the southern Italian grape Fiano is zippier than it used to be—crisp and zesty rather than soft and fruity. Still great value.

Stockists: *Almost nationwide* Dunnes Stores

Kiwi Cuvée Sauvignon Blanc Vin de Pays du Val de Loire

Loire Valley, France
€6.99

Vintage: 2007
Grape: Sauvignon Blanc
Alcohol: 11.5%
Plus point: Screwcap; among 10 Best Recession-Busters, page 13
Food matches: Aperitif; salads; delicate fish or seafood (with or without an Asian twist); Thai green curries

Clever, this. French and New Zealand winemakers join forces to produce a Sauvignon Blanc which combines classic Loire crispness with the riper, more generous flavours typical of NZ. Delicious. And look at that price. . .

Stockists: *Almost nationwide* Eurospar; Mace; Spar

La Basca Verdejo

Castilla y León, North-West Spain
€9.49

Vintage: 2007
Grape: Verdejo
Alcohol: 12.5%
Food matches: Aperitif; many light foods—salads; fish; shellfish; chicken (especially spicy chicken wings); omelettes; green-vegetable-based dishes

The Verdejo grape is on a roll—maybe because it offers Sauvignon Blanc-like exuberance with a little more body and substance. This tasty version is made by superstar winemaker Telmo Rodriguez and it shows.

Stockists: *Almost nationwide* Marks & Spencer

Fish Hoek

Allied Drinks Distributors Ltd
24 Parkwest Enterprise Centre, Nangor Road, Dublin 12 Tel: 01 642 9000

La Croix Gratiot Picpoul de Pinet Coteaux du Languedoc ★

Languedoc, South of France
€11.99

Vintage: 2007
Grape: Picpoul Blanc
Alcohol: 12.5%
Food matches: Aperitif (summer especially); salads; sardines; mackerel; fish and chips; omelettes

Who says the South of France can't produce tongue-tingling whites? The little-known grape Picpoul delivers terrific, lemony vigour—but rarely with as much smooth charm, harmony and intensity of flavour as here.

Stockists: *Mail order* wineonline.ie **Dublin** *64 Wine, Glasthule; Enowine, IFSC & Monkstown; Donnybrook Fair, Donnybrook; Lilac Wines, Fairview; Malt House, James St* **Waterford** *Florries Wines, Tramore*

Marks & Spencer Mâcon-Villages

Southern Burgundy, France
€10.49

Vintage: 2007
Grape: Chardonnay
Alcohol: 13%
Plus point: Screwcap; among 10 Best Wines for a Big Party, page 66
Food matches: Aperitif; salads; fish including salmon; crab or
prawns; chicken pie; light vegetarian dishes; cheese dishes

So brilliantly versatile and subtly appealing
is this gentle, unoaked white Burgundy
that it suggests the (late) Chardonnay
craze was driven partly by that grape's
superb adaptability to food. Smooth and
lemony, it has a little bit of body but no
flab.

Stockists: *Almost nationwide* Marks & Spencer

Mitchelton Blackwood Park Riesling

Central Victoria, Australia
€9.99

Vintage: 2006
Grape: Riesling
Alcohol: 13.5%
Plus point: Screwcap; among 10 Best Wines for a Big Party, page 66
Food matches: Aperitif; light salads; dim sum; spring rolls; light fish, seafood or chicken dishes (especially with an Asian twist)

Try this gentle Riesling alongside a Chinese, Indian or Thai takeaway with delicate spice and limited chilli burn. Before you know it, the bottle will be half empty. Floral and quite fruity with a refreshing streak of citrus, it's the essence of easy drinking.

Stockists: *Almost nationwide* Dunnes Stores

Wine Australia
www.wineaustralia.com

Ballyvaughan
Co Clare

T. 065 7077264

ireland@wineaustralia.com

Montana East Coast Unoaked Chardonnay

North Island, New Zealand
€11.99

Vintage: 2006
Grape: Chardonnay
Alcohol: 13%
Plus point: Screwcap
Food matches: Very versatile—aperitif; salads; fish or seafood; chicken; pork; omelette; cheese soufflé. . . almost anything light

There's a refreshing, citrussy lift to this well-crafted Chardonnay that lingers impressively, prepping the tastebuds for the next mouthful. Understated but likeable, it will suit many different dishes (and different drinkers, too).

Stockists: *Almost nationwide Dunnes Stores; Superquinn; SuperValu/Centra;Tesco; and many independent off-licences countrywide*

Peter Lehmann Barossa Riesling

Barossa Valley, South Australia
€9.99

Vintage: 2006
Grape: Riesling
Alcohol: 12.5%
Plus point: Screwcap; among 10 Best Wines for Spicy Foods,
page 41
Food matches: Aperitif; fish; seafood; chicken; Thai green curries;
mild to medium-spicy Indian and Chinese dishes

Lehmann's gifted winemaker (and Riesling fan) Andrew Wigan has the knack of packing terrific lime intensity into this bargain bottle. The result is a brilliantly versatile wine which copes well with pungent flavours. It ages well, too.

Stockists: *Dublin* Bennetts, Howth; Donnybrook Fair; Eurospar, Rathcoole; Jus de Vine, Portmarnock; Molloys outlets; Red Island, Skerries; Redmonds, Ranelagh; Unwined, Swords; Vintry, Rathgar **Galway** Vineyard, Galway **Kildare** Applegreen, Newbridge; Mill Wine Cellar, Maynooth **Meath** Bunch of Grapes, Clonee; Next Door, Enfield **Roscommon** Dalys, Boyle **Tipperary** Lonergans, Clonmel **Waterford** Ardkeen Stores, Waterford **Wicklow** Hollands, Bray

Petit Bourgeois Sauvignon Blanc ★
Vin de Pays du Val de Loire

Loire Valley, France
€11.99

Vintage: 2007
Grape: Sauvignon Blanc
Alcohol: 12%
Food matches: Aperitif; many salads and light first courses; delicate shellfish or white fish; goat's cheese. Fresh herbs will help the match.

Well-known Sancerre producer Henri Bourgeois has created this zippy cousin of Sancerre at two-thirds of the price. With all the cool 'green' notes you'd expect— gooseberries, nettles, herbs, summer grass—it's delightfully crisp but not austere.

Stockists: *Almost nationwide* O'Briens

Schloss Schönborn Riesling Trocken ★

Rheingau, Germany
€11.49

Vintage: 2007
Grape: Riesling
Alcohol: 12.5%
Plus point: Screwcap; among 10 Bottles Most Likely to Impress a Wine Buff, page 118
Food matches: Aperitif; ham, pork or chicken (especially with apples or with a honey glaze); onion tart; or by itself any time

If this elegant, exquisitely balanced wine doesn't encourage you to explore the neglected but exciting world of German Riesling, nothing will. It's dry, crisp and reviving without being tart, thanks to a fine vein of honey all the way through.

Stockists: *Almost nationwide* O'Briens

Tesco Finest Gavi

Piedmont, North-West Italy
€9.99

Vintage: 2007
Grape: Cortese
Alcohol: 12.5%
Food matches: Aperitif; fish or shellfish; light chicken dishes; lemon or green vegetable risottos; tomato-based pasta dishes

Here is another very smart Gavi at a knockdown price. Alongside smooth pear, peach and lemon notes you'll find a kind of wet-stone character and a zesty, yeasty edge—both of them essential to Gavi's lively charm.

Stockists: *Almost nationwide* Tesco

Tesco Finest Steillage Riesling

Mosel Valley, Germany
€10.99

Vintage: 2006
Grape: Riesling
Alcohol: 11%
Plus point: Screwcap
Food matches: Aperitif; ham, pork or chicken (especially with apples or a honey glaze); onion tart; lightly spiced Chinese chicken or pork dishes; or by itself

I absolutely love this wine. Like all the best German Rieslings it dances with vigour, packing extraordinarily vibrant flavours (ripe apples, lemon, honey) into its slender body. An anytime treat—and it tastes just as seductive the next day.

Stockists: *Almost nationwide* Tesco

Tesco Finest Tingleup Vineyard Riesling

Great Southern, Western Australia
€10.99

Vintage: 2007
Grape: Riesling
Alcohol: 13%
Plus point: Screwcap; among 10 Best Wines for Christmas, page 133
Food matches: Aperitif; salads; seafood or fish (especially with an Asian twist); light Chinese, Indian or Thai dishes

Rarely has a vineyard been so aptly named, for this Riesling is a real tongue-tingler. Lime sherbet and fresh lime flavours fan out to reveal slatey minerality underneath. Very stylish indeed, as might be expected of top Riesling producer Howard Park.

Stockists: *Almost nationwide* Tesco

Wine Australia
www.wineaustralia.com

Ballyvaughan
Co Clare

T. 065 7077264

ireland@wineaustralia.com

The Beach House
Sauvignon Blanc-Sémillon

Western Cape, South Africa
€9.99

Vintage: 2007
Grape: Sauvignon Blanc, Sémillon
Alcohol: 12%
Plus point: Screwcap
Food matches: Aperitif; salads (especially with fennel or herbs); fish; seafood; Thai green curries; goat's cheese

The starfish label may be like a gaudy beach accessory, but look beyond it. You'll find a smashing wine with gooseberry and lime juiciness. . . perked up by the tang of fresh herbs. A rival to the smart whites of Australia's Margaret River at half the price.

Stockists: *Almost nationwide* Dunnes Stores

Tramoya Rueda Verdejo

Rueda, North-West Spain
€7.99

Vintage: 2007
Grape: Verdejo
Alcohol: 13%
Plus point: Among 10 Best Recession-Busters, page 13
Food matches: Aperitif; versatile—salads; fish; shellfish; chicken (especially spicy chicken wings); Thai green curries; tomato or green-vegetable-based dishes

Another wine whose sheer verve and tastiness defy all attempts to explain its rock-bottom price. I've enjoyed it through several vintages and it retains the same zingy gooseberry flavour mixed with tropical fruit tones and an earthy, artisanal edge.

Stockists: *Almost nationwide* Dunnes Stores

Vansha Sauvignon Blanc

Paarl, South Africa
€9.49

Vintage: 2007
Grape: Sauvignon Blanc
Alcohol: 13.5%
Plus point: Screwcap
Food matches: Aperitif; many light seafood, salad, chicken or vegetable dishes; Thai green curries; creamy pastas

Half way between New Zealand and the Loire (stylistically if not quite geographically), South Africa is producing some superb Sauvignons—like this. Pure grapefruit allure with cool zestiness and a hint of smoky minerality tell the story.

Stockists: *Almost nationwide* Superquinn

Viña Mar de Casablanca Sauvignon Blanc Reserva

Casablanca Valley, Chile
€9.99

Vintage: 2007
Grape: Sauvignon Blanc
Alcohol: 13%
Food matches: Aperitif; light salads; light fish and seafood dishes (including sushi and delicate curries); pasta with pesto

While researching this book I sampled more Chilean Sauvignon Blanc than any other sort of wine. Many were mediocre to middling—or tasty but priced at €11.99. With its citrussy purity, depth and evenness, this one definitely offers more for less.

Stockists: *Almost nationwide* Superquinn

Winzer Krems Grüner Veltliner Ried Sandgrube

Kremstal, Austria
€11.99

Vintage: 2007
Grape: Grüner Veltliner
Alcohol: 12.5%
Food matches: Aperitif; salads (especially with pears); light fish dishes; scallops; cold chicken

Increasingly fashionable Grüner Veltliner— Austria's white speciality grape—produces wines ranging from crisp and delicate to full-bodied and assertive. This light, zippy, pear-toned version is guaranteed to get the appetite in gear.

Stockists: *Dublin* *Corkscrew, Chatham St; Gibney's, Malahide; Hole in the Wall, Blackhorse Ave; Redmond's, Ranelagh; Spar, Carpenterstown* ***Galway*** *Cases Wine Warehouse, Galway;* ***Meath*** *Coolers, Ongar Village nr Clonee* ***Wicklow*** *Wicklow Arms,Delgany*

MORE
FULL-BODIED
WHITES

Angosto Valencia

Valencia, Central Spain
€11.99

Vintage: 2007
Grape: Moscatel, Verdejo, Sauvignon Blanc, Chardonnay
Alcohol: 12.5%
Food matches: Aperitif; melon or other fruity first courses; ham; light Thai dishes; goat's cheese tarts

Made from an exotic cocktail of grape varieties, here's a white wine with attitude. Smooth, suave and assertive, it exudes all those green fruits you might put into a summer fruit salad—melon, lime zest, pears, muscat grapes and more. Wow!

Stockists: *Mail order* www.spanishwines.ie

De Wetshof Danie De Wet Chardonnay Sur Lie

Robertson, South Africa
€11.99

Vintage: 2006
Grape: Chardonnay
Alcohol: 14%
Plus point: Screwcap
Food matches: Needs food—Caesar salad; baked ham; roast chicken or pork; chicken satay; chicken, pork or vegetable stir-fries; potato gratin

From one of South Africa's most talented winemakers, this lovely, lemony wine derives its creamy texture and round body not from oak but from a spell on the yeast lees after fermentation. A great food wine. It's bone-dry.

Stockists: *Donegal* *Next Door, Killybegs* ***Dublin*** *Corkscrew, Chatham St; Jus de Vine, Portmarnock; Sweeneys, Glasnevin* **Kildare** *O'Rourkes, Newbridge* **Meath** *Bunch of Grapes, Clonee; Next Door, Enfield*

Dolle Grüner Veltliner Strassertal

Kamptal, Austria
€9.99

Vintage: 2006
Grape: Grüner Veltliner
Alcohol: 12.5%
Plus point: Screwcap; among 10 Bottles Most Likely to Impress a Wine Buff, page 118
Food matches: Aperitif; salads (especially with pears); scallops; roast pork with apple sauce; pork stir-fry; cheese fondue

Considering that it is made from a newly fashionable and often relatively expensive grape variety, this wine represents outstanding value. It starts off fresh and tangy with typical pear and yeasty notes, then opens out to become surprisingly mouthfilling.

Stockists: *Almost nationwide* Superquinn

Les Perles Viognier Vin de Pays d'Oc

Languedoc, South of France
€11.50

Vintage: 2006
Grape: Viognier
Alcohol: 13%
Food matches: Aperitif; crab or prawns; pork with apricots;
honey-glazed chicken or ham; light Chinese dishes; vegetable
biryani

Among the many Viogniers tasted for this
book, here is the undisputed star. Why?
Because it has striking freshness and
delicacy, alongside the heady floral and
peach notes that are so typical of this
intriguing grape. Too many are heavy and
overblown.

Stockists: *Clare Egans Wines, Liscannor* **Cork** *Karwig,
Carrigaline* **Dublin** *64 Wine, Glasthule; Gibneys,
Malahide; Michaels Wines, Mount Merrion; Mitchell
& Son, CHQ Building IFSC, Glasthule & Rathfarnham;
Sweeneys, Glasnevin; Unwined, Swords* **Kerry** *Kingdom Stores, Tralee*
Waterford *Ardkeen Stores, Waterford*

Louis Latour Ardèche Chardonnay

Southern Rhône Valley, France
€11.50

Vintage: 2006
Grape: Chardonnay
Alcohol: 13%
Plus point: Aged in barrels previously used for ritzy Corton-
Charlemagne; among 10 Best Wines for Christmas, page 133
Food matches: Needs substantial food—smoked fish; fish pie or fish
in a cream sauce; roast chicken; roast pork; cheese gratin

Although I've liked this wine for years, it took a visit to the Ardèche winery of Burgundy producer Latour to realise how carefully it is made and how well it ages. Rich and round, it has a lovely savoury character—slightly nutty, almost salty.

Stockists: ***Dublin*** *Cheers Take Home, Liffey Valley; Coolers, Ongar Village; Corks, Terenure; Nolans, Clontarf; Quinns, Drumcondra; Savages, Swords; Silver Granite, Palmerstown* ***Clare*** *Jaynes, Ennis* ***Galway*** *Harvest outlets* ***Waterford*** *Flynns Bar & Off Licence, Waterford* ***Wicklow*** *Quinns, Baltinglass*

Marks & Spencer Langhe Arneis

Piedmont, North-West Italy

€10.50

Vintage: 2007
Grape: Arneis
Alcohol: 13%
Plus point: Screwcap
Food matches: Aperitif; mixed antipasti; smoked fish; roast chicken
(especially with lemon)

Full marks to Marks for sussing out such an attractive version of Italy's unusual Arneis grape. Subtly scented with pear, apricot and honey, this medium-bodied wine unfurls in the mouth, its fruity nature kept in check by a juicy undertow of lemon.

Stockists: *Almost nationwide* Marks & Spencer

Mitchelton Thomas Mitchell Marsanne

South-Eastern Australia
€8.49

Vintage: 2007
Grape: Marsanne
Alcohol: 12.5%
Plus point: Screwcap; among 10 Best Wines for Spicy Foods, page 41
Food matches: Hot Thai soups; spicy crab cakes; creamy chicken or vegetable curries; chicken satay; chicken or pork stir-fries; vegetable biryani

With its heady tropical notes—pineapple, mangoes, lime—and a streak of honey, Australian Marsanne takes some getting used to. The trick is to make it shine with the right food (see above). Less alcoholic than many, this one slips down all too easily.

Stockists: *Almost nationwide Dunnes Stores*

Wine Australia
www.wineaustralia.com

Ballyvaughan
Co Clare

T. 065 7077264

ireland@wineaustralia.com

10 best wines for spicy foods

Sparkling
- Jacob's Creek Sparkling Rosé Dry Cuvée
  €13.99 (page 136)

White
- Peter Lehmann Barossa Riesling
  €9.99 (page 22)
- Mitchelton Thomas Mitchell Marsanne
  €8.49 (page 40)
- Tesco Finest Ken Forrester Chenin Blanc
  €11.49 (page 45)

Rosé
- Miguel Torres Santa Digna Cabernet Sauvignon Rosé
  €10.99 (page 55)

Red
- Botalcura Syrah-Malbec Reserva El Delirio
  €11.95 (page 82)
- Carmen Syrah
  €9.99 (page 83)
- Flagstone Fish Hoek Shiraz
  €9.99 (page 99)
- La Ferme du Mont 'Le Ponnant' Côtes du Rhône Villages
  €10.99–€11.99 (page 103)
- Trapiche Oak Cask Pinot Noir
  €9.99 (page 75)

Monte del Frà Custoza

Veneto, North-East Italy
€10.95

Vintage: 2006
Grape: Garganega
Alcohol: 12%
Food matches: Aperitif; mixed antipasti; melon (especially with Parma ham); chicken risotto; pork with orange

Smelling this wine is like diving into a fruit salad of orange and grapefruit with a squeeze of lemon. It tastes a little that way too, with a smooth, creamy texture which makes the wine feel mouthfilling but not in the least heavy. Different and delicious.

Stockists: *Mail order* www.bbr.ie **Dublin** *Berry Bros & Rudd, Harry St*

Simone Joseph Chardonnay ★
Vin de Pays

South of France
€11.95

Vintage: 2007
Grape: Chardonnay
Alcohol: 13.5%
Plus point: Among 10 Best Wines for a Posh Dinner, page 49; also 10 Best Wines for Christmas, page 133
Food matches: Very versatile—aperitif; Caesar salad; fish; seafood; chicken; pork; ham; cheese or egg-based dishes; vegetable or cheese and potato gratins

If you've been suffering from a touch of Chardonnay fatigue, this pristine example will send it packing. (And faithful Chardonnay fans will be in heaven.) Exquisitely fresh melon, peach and lemon tones come with body and superb staying power.

Stockists: Cork *Kitchen Project, Cork* **Dublin** *Drink Store, Manor St; Jus de Vine, Portmarnock; McCabes, Blackrock; Redmonds, Ranelagh* **Galway** *Cases, Galway* **Kerry** *Vanilla Grape, Kenmare*

Tahbilk Nagambie Lakes Marsanne ★

Central Victoria, Australia
€11.99

Vintage: 2006
Grape: Marsanne
Alcohol: 13%
Plus point: Screwcap; among 10 Bottles Most Likely to Impress a Wine Buff, page 118
Food matches: Good with spicy (even red-hot) foods—Thai soups; spicy crab cakes; seafood, chicken or vegetable curries; chicken satay

This luscious Marsanne is one of Australia's icon wines. From the largest, oldest Marsanne vineyard in the world (planted in 1927), it has glorious pineapple, peach and honey tones. After a few years it develops an extra layer of smoky richness.

Stockists: ***Dublin*** *Bennetts, Howth; Deveneys, Dundrum; Donnybrook Fair; Drink Store, Manor St; Eurospar, Rathcoole; Gibneys, Malahide; Goose, Drumcondra; Higgins, Clonskeagh; Jus de Vine, Portmarnock; Mortons, Ranelagh; O'Neills, SC Rd; Redmonds, Ranelagh; Unwined, Swords; Vintry, Rathgar* ***Galway*** *Vineyard, Galway* ***Kildare*** *Mill Wine Cellar, Maynooth* ***Roscommon*** *Dalys, Boyle* ***Wicklow*** *Hollands, Bray; Wicklow Arms, Delgany*

Tesco Finest Ken Forrester Chenin Blanc

Stellenbosch, South Africa
€11.49

Vintage: 2007
Grape: Chenin Blanc
Alcohol: 13.5%
Plus point: Screwcap; among 10 Best Wines for Spicy Foods, page 41
Food matches: Salads with fruit, or with an Asian touch; chicken or vegetable curries; chicken, pork or vegetable stir-fries; roast pork with apricots or apple

Ken Forrester, the man who makes this amply fruity, honey-streaked, personality-packed wine, is mad about South Africa's old Chenin Blanc bush vines. His Chenin is listed in Gordon Ramsay in London and Spago in Beverly Hills. Need we say more?

Stockists: *Almost nationwide* Tesco

Tesco Finest Oak-Aged White Burgundy

Burgundy, France
€10.99

Vintage: 2007
Grape: Chardonnay
Alcohol: 13%
Plus point: Screwcap
Food matches: Most kinds of fish (including smoked); most chicken dishes; baked ham; many pork dishes; cheese and egg-based dishes

Oaked Chardonnay triggers such a negative response these days that you may shudder at the mere thought. But, believe me, the oak influence here is really subtle— just plumping out this smooth, tasty wine a shade. Perfect judgment.

Stockists: *Almost nationwide* Tesco

ROSÉS

Artazuri Navarra Garnacha Rosado

Navarra, North-East Spain
€11.95

Vintage: 2007
Grape: Garnacha
Alcohol: 13.5%
Plus point: Screwcap; among 10 Best Wines for a Posh Dinner, page 49
Food matches: Aperitif; tapas; grilled tuna; barbecued meats; tomato-based dishes; tandoori chicken and other spicy dishes

Made with fastidious care by Bodegas Artadi, better known for their top-drawer Riojas, this rosé positively bounces with life. It's flavoursome enough to stand up to a vast array of punchy foods.

Stockists: *Mail order* www.jnwine.com *Dublin Corkscrew, Chatham St; Drink Store, Manor St; Goggins, Monkstown; Martins, Marino; Michaels Wines, Mount Merrion* **Galway** *Guys Wine Shop, Galway; Mortons, Salthill* **Mayo** *Fahys, Ballina*

10 best wines for a posh dinner

Sparkling

- Guerrieri-Rizzardi Prosecco Vino Spumante Extra Dry
  €14.99 (page 134)

White

- Chateau des Eyssards Bergerac Sec
  €9.80 (page 6)
- Devil's Corner Sauvignon Blanc
  €11.99 (page 9)
- Simone Joseph Chardonnay Vin de Pays
  €11.95 (page 43)

Rosé

- Artazuri Navarra Garnacha Rosado
  €11.95 (page 48)

Red

- Chateau de Bayle Bordeaux
  €11.95 (page 85)
- Domaine Grès Saint Vincent Côtes du Rhône Villages Sinargues
  €10.99 (page 91)
- Poggio del Sasso Sangiovese di Toscana
  €11.99 (page 111)
- Raimat Abadia Crianza
  €10.99 (page 72)
- Secano Estate Pinot Noir
  €10.99 (page 74)

Chivite Gran Feudo Navarra Rosado

Navarra, North-East Spain
€9.99

Vintage: 2007
Grape: Garnacha
Alcohol: 13%
Plus point: Screwcap; among 10 Best Recession-Busters, page 13
Food matches: Versatile—aperitif; salads; prawns; crab; salmon; chicken or pork (Asian or otherwise); stuffed red peppers

One of the least expensive rosés in this book and it offers better value than ever. The price hasn't changed in seven years—nor has the quality. Fresh, fruity and engaging with a reviving rhubarb tang in the finish.

Stockists: *Almost nationwide Dunnes Stores; Next Door outlets; O'Briens; Superquinn; and many independent off-licences countrywide* **Cork** *O'Donovans outlets and many other independents* **Dublin** *Molloys outlets and many other independents*

Domaine Bégude Pinot Rosé ★
Vin de Pays d'Oc

Languedoc, South of France
€9.99

Vintage: 2007
Grape: Pinot Noir
Alcohol: 12%
Plus point: Screwcap; biodynamically grown grapes; among 10 Best Wines for a Big Party, page 66
Food matches: Aperitif; salads (especially tomato); prawns; cold salmon; cold meats; also delicious by itself

This pale salmon-pink rosé no doubt owes its freshness and delicacy to the cool situation of the vineyards, in the French Pyrenees near Limoux. Fragrant strawberry aromas, wonderfully pure flavours. . . a truly stylish treat.

Stockists: *Almost nationwide* Superquinn

Domaine Clavel Mescladis Rosé Coteaux du Languedoc

Languedoc, South of France
€10.75

Vintage: 2007
Grape: Syrah, Cinsault
Alcohol: 13%
Food matches: Aperitif; tapas or antipasti; salmon; tuna—grilled or in salade nicoise; ham; spicy fish, chicken or pork dishes

The smell of strawberries and freshly poached rhubarb wafts from the glass, immediately giving this lively, moreish rosé a summery feel. But it is assertive enough in style for year-round enjoyment with all sorts of dishes.

Stockists: *Mail order* www.winesdirect.ie

Errazuriz Estate Cabernet Sauvignon Rosé

Central Valley, Chile
€10.99

Vintage: 2007
Grape: Cabernet Sauvignon
Alcohol: 13%
Plus point: Screwcap
Food matches: Best with flavoursome food—rustic patés; chicken, duck or pork—roast, barbecued or Chinese-style; spicy vegetable couscous

The deep crimson colour is the first clue that this is what I'd describe as a swaggering rosé. With vibrant blackcurrant and raspberry overtones and a peppery flourish, it's made for foods with robust flavours—not solo sipping.

Stockists: *Almost nationwide* *Dunnes Stores; Next Door; Superquinn; SuperValu/Centra* **Cork** *O'Donovans outlets* **Dublin** *McHughs, Artane & Kilbarrack; Mitchell & Son, CHQ Building IFSC, Glasthule & Rathfarnham; Molloys outlets; Mortons, Ranelagh; Redmonds, Ranelagh; Vintry, Rathgar* **Wicklow** *Wicklow Wine Co, Wicklow*

Guerrieri-Rizzardi Rosa Rosae Rosato ★

Veneto, North-East Italy
€11.99

Vintage: 2007
Grape: Corvina, Rondinella, Sangiovese
Alcohol: 12.5%
Food matches: Aperitif; mixed antipasti; prawns; salmon; tuna; prosciutto, salami and other cold meats—even turkey post-Christmas

Like an acrobat on a tightrope, this supremely elegant rosé is perfectly poised at the mid-point between delicacy and full power. A terrific appetite stimulant, it has a lovely, gentle persistence—its refined flavours linger magically.

Stockists: *Almost nationwide* O'Briens

Allied Drinks Distributors Ltd
24 Parkwest Enterprise Centre, Nangor Road, Dublin 12
Tel: 01 642 9000

ERRAZURIZ

Miguel Torres Santa Digna Cabernet Sauvignon Rosé Reserve

Central Valley, Chile
€10.99

Vintage: 2007
Grape: Cabernet Sauvignon
Alcohol: 14%
Plus point: Screwcap; among 10 Best Wines for Spicy Foods, page 41
Food matches: Best with main courses—chicken (including tandoori or balti); duck breasts (spicy or not); Asian pork dishes; pasta with tomato sauce

This confident rosé from the Torres Chilean winery is much brawnier than its Spanish cousin (page 58)—but give it gutsy food and it won't seem OTT. In fact, its ripe red fruit flavours are a positive boon with spices in the medium-hot zone.

Stockists: *Almost nationwide Londis; Next Door; SuperValu/Centra* **Dublin** *Cheers outlets; McCabes, Blackrock; Mitchell & Son, CHQ Building IFSC, Glasthule & Rathfarnham; Molloys outlets*

Petit Bourgeois Rosé de Pinot Noir ★ Vin de Pays

Loire Valley, France
€11.99

Vintage: 2007
Grape: Pinot Noir
Alcohol: 12.5%
Plus point: Among 10 Bottles Most Likely to Impress a Wine Buff, page 118
Food matches: Aperitif; many light first courses—salads (tomato especially); prawns; poached salmon; charcuterie; light, creamy cheeses

Henri Bourgeois strikes again (see page 23)—this time with a light-footed pink that bears more than a passing resemblance to swish Sancerre rosé. Smelling and tasting like Pink Lady Apples, it's pure to the power of ten and brilliantly enticing.

Stockists: *Almost nationwide* O'Briens

Principe de Viana Navarra Cabernet Sauvignon Rosado ★

Navarra, North-East Spain
€11.99

Vintage: 2007
Grape: Cabernet Sauvignon
Alcohol: 12.5%
Food matches: Aperitif; many middle-weight dishes including grilled chicken; pork kebabs; duck breasts; stuffed red peppers

The almost crimson colour is the first clue that this peppy rosé has more body and stuffing than most. With layers of tangy red fruit flavours—strawberries, rhubarb, redcurrants—it's wonderfully invigorating but a little too sharp for spicy foods.

Stockists: *Cork* O'Donovans outlets *Dublin* Bin No. 9, Goatstown; Donnybrook Fair, Donnybrook; Gibneys, Malahide; McCabes, Blackrock & Foxrock; Sweeneys, Glasnevin; Thomas Deli, Foxrock *Kerry* Kingdom Stores, Tralee

Torres de Casta Rosada

Catalunya, North-East Spain
€9.99

Vintage: 2007
Grape: Garnacha, Cariñena
Alcohol: 13%
Plus point: Screwcap
Food matches: Aperitif; very versatile—salads, tapas or other light starters; cold meats; pizzas and many pasta dishes

I've long admired Torres—Spain's largest family-owned wine company—for its ability to produce attractive wines at modest prices. This rosé is a prime example. So vibrant are the fresh fruit flavours that you feel you can almost bite into them.

Stockists: *Almost nationwide Dunnes Stores; Next Door; Superquinn* **Dublin** *McCabes, Blackrock; Molloys outlets*

ELEGANT, MEDIUM-BODIED REDS

Agustinos Pinot Noir Reserva

Bio Bio Valley, Chile
€9.99

Vintage: 2007
Grape: Pinot Noir
Alcohol: 14%
Food matches: Roast or grilled chicken; baked ham; duck breasts; grilled lamb cutlets

One of three wines in this section which prove that Chile has mastered the art of producing very smart Pinot Noir at an unbeatable price. This one combines the juicy flavours of soft red summer fruits with gentle spice and underlying firmness.

Stockists: ***Almost nationwide*** *Superquinn*

Antinori Santa Cristina Toscana

Tuscany, Central Italy
€10.50

Vintage: 2006
Grape: Sangiovese, Merlot
Alcohol: 13%
Food matches: Spaghetti Bolognese or lasagne; grilled chicken or sausages; beef carpaccio or cold roast beef; pizza or pasta with tomato sauce

The clever old house of Antinori created this brilliantly successful blend in 1984 by smoothing out the bitter cherry rasp of Sangiovese with a dollop of soft Merlot. It's still a winner—round, juicy and likeable with the earthy edge of a 'real' wine.

Stockists: *Almost nationwide Dunnes Stores; O'Briens; SuperValu/Centra* **Cork** *Bradleys, Cork* **Dublin** *Molloys outlets; Redmonds, Ranelagh* **Galway** *Joyces, Galway & Headford* **Waterford** *Ardkeen Stores, Waterford*

Berrys' Good Ordinary Claret

Bordeaux, France
€11.95

Vintage: 2005
Grape: Merlot, Cabernet Sauvignon
Alcohol: 13%
Food matches: Roast or grilled chicken; mixed grill; better still with duck; lamb; beef

A big step up in quality and charm from earlier versions of this Berrys' stalwart which had become Ordinary rather than Good. Smooth, concentrated and blackcurranty with that 'pencil lead' mineral streak which is so typical of Bordeaux.

Stockists: *Mail order www.bbr.ie* **Dublin** *Berry Bros & Rudd, Harry St*

Chivite Gran Feudo Navarra Crianza

Navarra, North-East Spain
€9.50

Vintage: 2004
Grape: Tempranillo, Garnacha, Cabernet Sauvignon
Alcohol: 12.5%
Food matches: Needs meaty flavours—roast or grilled lamb or beef; peppered steak; baked aubergines

If you like big, ripe, modern, alcoholic reds, this model of savoury elegance is not for you. But if you enjoy classic wines with the alluring touch of leathery complexity that maturity brings, you'll love one of the wine world's most enduring bargains.

Stockists: *Almost nationwide Dunnes Stores; Next Door outlets; O'Briens; Superquinn; and many independent off-licences countrywide* **Cork** *O'Donovans outlets and many other independents* **Dublin** *Mollys outlets and many other independents*

Cono Sur Pinot Noir

Central Valley, Chile
€8.99–€9.99

Vintage: 2007
Grape: Pinot Noir
Alcohol: 14%
Plus point: Screwcap; among 10 Best Wines for a Big Party, page 66
Food matches: Roast or grilled chicken; baked ham; lamb cutlets;
duck breasts; cheese or vegetable dishes; also fine without food

If you serve this with food, try to work in a
sprinkling of herbs to echo the attractive
herbal notes in this yummy Pinot Noir. Lavish
flavours of loganberries and other red fruits
segue into a firm, dry, lasting finish.

Stockists: *Almost nationwide* Londis; O'Briens;
SuperValu/Centra **Cork** Bradleys, Cork; O'Donovans
outlets **Donegal** Next Door, Killybegs **Dublin** Baily
Wines, Howth; Bennetts, Howth; Cellars Big Wine
Warehouse, Naas Rd; Coach House, Ballinteer; Coolers,
Applewood; Jus de Vine, Portmarnock; Molloys outlets;
Redmonds, Ranelagh **Galway** Harvest outlets; Joyces,
Galway & Headford **Meath** Bunch of Grapes, Clonee; Carrolls, Kells;
Next Door, Enfield **Tipperary** Coopers, Tipperary; Eldons, Clonmel
Waterford Ardkeen Stores, Waterford

Corinto Merlot

Central Valley, Chile
€8.95

Vintage: 2006
Grape: Merlot
Alcohol: 12.5%
Plus point: Screwcap; among 10 Best Wines for a Big Party, page 66
Food matches: Versatile—poultry of all kinds; meat of all kinds; cheese or flavoursome vegetable dishes; also fine without food

Chilean Merlot is so often merely average that I rarely recommend it. But this is a real beauty. Although it offers plenty of flavour (damson or plum liqueur notes with a pinch of thyme), it comes with a touch of elegant restraint. And what a great price!

Stockists: *Almost nationwide* Next Door **Dublin** *Fallon & Byrne, Exchequer St; On the Grapevine, Booterstown; Red Island Wines, Skerries; Searsons, Monkstown; Uncorked, Rathfarnham* **Meath** *Cashel Wine Cellar, Navan* **Sligo** *Patrick Stewart Wines, Sligo* **Waterford** *Oskars Wine Shop, Waterford*

10 best wines for a big (but ritzy) party

Sparkling
- Marks & Spencer Prosecco Raboso Rosé Spumante Brut
  €12.49 (page 137)

White
- Château Pique-Sègue Montravel
  €9.99 (page 7)
- Flying Kiwi Marlborough Sauvignon Blanc
  €9.99 (page 11)
- Marks & Spencer Mâcon-Villages
  €10.49 (page 18)
- Mitchelton Blackwood Park Riesling
  €9.99 (page 19)

Rosé
- Domaine Bégude Pinot Rosé Vin de Pays d'Oc
  €9.99 (page 51)

Red
- Cono Sur Pinot Noir
  €8.99–€9.99 (page 64)
- Corinto Merlot
  €8.95 (page 65)
- Domaine Lafond Roc-Épine Côtes du Rhône
  €10.99 (page 92)
- T'Air d'Oc Syrah Vin de Pays d'Oc
  €10.95 (page 117)

Flying Kiwi South Island Pinot Noir

South Island, New Zealand
€11.99

Vintage: 2007
Grape: Pinot Noir
Alcohol: 13%
Plus point: Screwcap
Food matches: Cold meats; ham, pork, lamb, chicken—cooked traditionally or in medium-spicy Indian or Chinese dishes

NZ Pinot Noir may be sexy, but by golly, most of it ain't cheap. So it's a treat to discover this fragrant, silky little number with its deliciously pure cherry and raspberry tones and lively tang. It comes from Belfast—near Christchurch, that is.

Stockists: *Almost nationwide* Eurospar; Mace; Spar

Marks & Spencer Bourgogne Pinot Noir 'Les Senteurs'

Burgundy, France
€10.99

Vintage: 2006
Grape: Pinot Noir
Alcohol: 13%
Food matches: Grilled foods—chicken; duck breasts; lamb cutlets; pork chops; chargrilled vegetables

There's a smoky overlay to this well-made, well-priced Burgundy that makes me want to light the barbecue. Medium-bodied and firm with a dash of spicy oak, it needs slightly more robust food than its M&S cousin on the next page.

Stockists: *Almost nationwide* Marks & Spencer

Marks & Spencer Mâcon Rouge

Burgundy, France
€10.49

Vintage: 2006
Grape: Gamay, Pinot Noir
Alcohol: 12.5%
Food matches: Versatile—salmon; tuna; cold chicken or cold meats; quesadillas; creamy cheeses; also fine by itself

This is what I'd call a pretty red wine— dainty, almost. Light, juicy and dangerously moreish, it has enticing aromas and flavours of fresh raspberries and strawberries with a pinch of herbs. Perfect for a summer lunch.

Stockists: *Almost nationwide* Marks & Spencer

Mitchell & Son Claret

Bordeaux, France
€11.50

Vintage: 2005
Grape: Merlot, Cabernet Sauvignon, Cabernet Franc
Alcohol: 13%
Food matches: Roast or grilled chicken; mixed grill; better still with duck; lamb; beef

Bordeaux now follows the New World recipe for voluptuousness a tad too slavishly, with the result that its reds can be souped up and soulless. Not this one. Although perfumed and ripe, it still has an unmistakeable Bordeaux identity. Well done.

Stockists: *Mail order* www.mitchellandson.com *Dublin Donohoes, College St; Mitchell & Son, CHQ Building IFSC, Glasthule & Rathfarnham Wexford Myles Doyles, Gorey*

Montana East Coast Merlot-Cabernet Sauvignon

North Island, New Zealand
€11.99

Vintage: 2006
Grape: Merlot, Cabernet Sauvignon
Alcohol: 13%
Plus point: Screwcap
Food matches: Versatile—chicken; most meats; many cheese or vegetable-based dishes; many pasta dishes

Harmony and judgment are the keynotes in this suave Bordeaux blend from New Zealand. Plummy flavours, subtle spice and a gentle squeeze of fine tannin all meld together seamlessly. It's very food-flexible, too.

Stockists: *Almost nationwide Dunnes Stores; O'Briens; Superquinn; SuperValu/Centra; Tesco; and many independent off-licences countrywide* **Dublin** *Molloys outlets*

Raimat Abadia Crianza ★

Costers del Segre, North-East Spain
€10.99

Vintage: 2005
Grape: Cabernet Sauvignon, Merlot, Tempranillo
Alcohol: 13.5%
Plus point: Among 10 Best Wines for a Posh Dinner, page 49
Food matches: Roast lamb or beef; chargrilled steak or hamburgers; flavoursome vegetarian dishes; mature, waxy cheeses

My admiration for this wine stretches back over years and in my eyes it's still a shining star. It has warm, plummy notes with a mature, savoury edge and a meat-friendly flourish of black pepper. I also love the silky texture.

Stockists: *Almost nationwide O'Briens*
Clare *Shannon Knights, Shannon* **Cork** *Bradleys, Cork* ***Dublin*** *Eurospar, Smithfield; Lilac Wines, Fairview; Sheils, Dorset St; Vintry, Rathgar* **Galway** *Joyces, Athenry* **Kilkenny** *Wine Centre, Kilkenny* **Laois** *Portlaoise Wine Vault, Portlaoise* **Meath** *Cashel Wine Cellar, Navan* **Tipperary** *Eldons, Clonmel* **Waterford** *Worldwide Wines, Waterford*

Rosso di Valpanera

Veneto, North-East Italy
€10.99

Vintage: 2005
Grape: Refosco, Cabernet Sauvignon, Merlot
Alcohol: 12.5%
Food matches: Good with fatty meats—ham, pork, charcuterie, sausages, duck; also mushroom dishes like risotto

The unusual red grape Refosco gives this wine its welcome individuality as well as a palate-cleansing tang. Light-to-medium in body, it has a core of juicy cherry flavours edged with liquorice. Slightly earthy overtones makes it a perfect mushroom match.

Stockists: *Clare Shannon Knights, Shannon* **Cork** *Lynchs, Glanmire* **Dublin** *Brackens, Glasnevin; Londis, Malahide; Martins, Fairview; Masseys Costcutter, Rathfarnham; Mortons, Firhouse; Sheils, Dorset St; SuperValu/Centra, Churchtown* **Louth** *Callans, Dundalk* **Meath** *Gardenworks, Dunboyne; Round O, Navan* **Wexford** *Reids, Enniscorthy* **Wicklow** *Hollands, Bray*

Secano Estate Pinot Noir ★

Leyda Valley, Chile
€10.99

Vintage: 2007
Grape: Pinot Noir
Alcohol: 14%
Plus point: Among 10 Best Wines for a Posh Dinner, page 49; also 10 Best Wines for Christmas, page 133
Food matches: Versatile—salmon; tuna; chicken; liver or liver paté; kidneys; pork; lamb; many cheese and vegetable-based dishes

You might wonder why a 14% alcohol wine is categorised as medium- rather than full-bodied, but this silky, super-juicy Pinot from cool Leyda is so light on its feet that it belongs here. Expect tantalising cherry notes with a faint puff of smoke.

Stockists: *Almost nationwide* Marks & Spencer

Trapiche Oak Cask Pinot Noir

Mendoza, Argentina
€9.99

Vintage: 2006
Grape: Pinot Noir
Alcohol: 13.5%
Plus point: Among 10 Best Wines for Spicy Foods, page 41
Food matches: Versatile—salmon; tuna; pork; lamb; chicken; duck;
vegetable dishes; stars with spicy versions of any of these

Soft, ripe, and round with just a hint of spice, this old favourite continues to be one of the best-value Pinots on the market. All the more impressive when you consider that only Argentina's coolest vineyards suit this finicky grape. A great all-rounder.

Stockists: *Dublin Bennetts, Howth; Bin No 9, Goatstown; Carvills, Camden St; Donnybrook Fair; Eurospar, Rathcoole; Goose, Drumcondra; Higgins, Clonskeagh; Jus de Vine, Portmarnock; Londis, Malahide; Martha's Vineyard, Rathfarnham; O'Neills, SC Rd; On the Grapevine, Booterstown & Dalkey; Orchard, Applewood; Red Island, Skerries; Redmonds, Ranelagh; Spar, Ballycullen & Rathcoole; Vintry, Rathgar* **Kildare** *Mill Wine Cellar, Maynooth* **Meath** *Bunch of Grapes, Clonee* **Roscommon** *Dalys, Boyle* **Tipperary** *Lonergans, Clonmel* **Wicklow** *Hollands, Bray*

Tyrrell's Old Winery Pinot Noir

South-Eastern Australia
€11.99

Vintage: 2006
Grape: Pinot Noir
Alcohol: 13%
Plus point: Screwcap
Food matches: Liver or kidneys; duck; roast chicken;
mushroom-based dishes; cheese dishes

Underneath its engaging aromas and
flavours of blackberries, plums and spice,
this well-judged Australian slowly reveals a
savoury, peppery aspect. The end-note is
gamey rather than fruity. Choose food to
suit and you will be rewarded.

Stockists: ***Almost nationwide*** *SuperValu/Centra; and other outlets*

Wine Australia
www.wineaustralia.com

Ballyvaughan
Co Clare

T. 065 7077264

ireland@wineaustralia.com

Yering Station Little Yering Pinot Noir ★

Yarra Valley, Victoria, Australia
€11.99

Vintage: 2006
Grape: Pinot Noir
Alcohol: 13%
Plus point: Screwcap; among 10 Bottles Most Likely to Impress a Wine Buff, page 118
Food matches: Liver or kidneys; duck; roast chicken; mushroom-based dishes; cheese dishes

From a producer with an outstanding Pinot Noir pedigree, this is a very smart wine. Purity of flavour is the first thing you'll notice; a lovely, juicy quality the second. There are gamey notes here too, leading to a firm, dry, savoury aftertaste.

Stockists: *Cork O'Donovans outlets* **Dublin** *Coach House, Ballinteer; Goose, Drumcondra; Jus de Vine, Portmarnock; McCabes, Blackrock & Foxrock; McHughs, Artane & Kilbarrack; Redmonds, Ranelagh* **Galway** *Salthill Liquor Store, Salthill* **Sligo** *Currids, Sligo* **Tipperary** *Kellers Take Home, Roscrea; Lonergans, Clonmel* **Waterford** *Worldwide Wines, Waterford* **Wicklow** *Capranis, Ashford; Hollands, Bray*

RICH, FULL-BODIED REDS

Altano Douro

Douro Valley, Portugal
€8.99

Vintage: 2005
Grape: Tinta Roriz, Touriga Franco
Alcohol: 13%
Plus point: Among 10 Best Recession-Busters, page 13
Food matches: Needs robust food—barbecued beef, sausages, spare ribs or kebabs; rich vegetarian stews

Made by the Symingtons, prominent port producers, this extrovert red shows why the Douro is being hailed as a source of exciting red wines. It's punchy, peppery, smoky and herbal all at once—with dense plum-prune flavours and slatey minerality.

Stockists: *Almost nationwide* O'Briens

Bestué de Otto Bestué Somontano Finca Rableros ★

Somontano, North-East Spain
€9.99

Vintage: 2005
Grape: Tempranillo, Cabernet Sauvignon
Alcohol: 13.5%
Plus point: Among 10 Bottles Most Likely to Impress a Wine Buff, page 118
Food matches: Red meats, roast or grilled; rich meat or vegetable casseroles; strong cheeses

This remarkable red bargain comes from an estate that has been in the Bestué family since 1640. Nicely mature with rich plum and blackberry flavours, a hint of smoke and a dusting of spice, it has a firm, meaty finish. A sophisticated wine.

Stockists: *Almost nationwide* Dunnes Stores

Bodega Norton Barrel Select Malbec

Mendoza, Argentina
€9.99

Vintage: 2005
Grape: Malbec
Alcohol: 13.5%
Food matches: Most meats (especially lamb or duck Asian-style); grilled aubergines; hearty vegetarian stew

Argentina is climbing high up my list of countries offering high quality at low prices—and Norton is among its star producers. Just try this polished Malbec. Round, juicy and subtly spicy, it smells like an autumn fruit fair. Damsons, blackberries, plums. . . mmmm.

Stockists: *Almost nationwide* O'Briens

www.approachwines.com

Dedication, passion, expertise, local knowledge – an unrivalled combination

Approach Trade

Botalcura Syrah-Malbec Reserva El Delirio

Central Valley, Chile
€11.95

Vintage: 2006
Grape: Syrah, Malbec
Alcohol: 14%
Plus point: Among 10 Best Wines for Spicy Foods, page 41
Food matches: Best with red meats and punchy red meat dishes—chilli con carne; beef goulasch; beef stir-fry; venison burgers

Although I'm wary of full-throttle reds (and ridiculously heavy bottles), this weighty attention-seeker is impressive. Heady aromas, lavish flavours and massive concentration—but there's a touch of freshness in there too (thank goodness).

Stockists: *Almost nationwide* Next Door **Dublin** *Donnybrook Fair, Donnybrook; Drink Store, Manor St; Mortons, Ranelagh; Searsons, Monkstown* **Galway** *Mortons, Salthill* **Kildare** *Swans on the Green, Naas* **Wicklow** *Emilias Fine Food & Wine, Enniskerry*

Carmen Syrah

Maipo Valley, Chile
€9.99

Vintage: 2006
Grape: Syrah
Alcohol: 13.5%
Plus point: Among 10 Best Wines for Spicy Foods, page 41
Food matches: Good with spicy meat dishes—chilli con carne; beef burritos; vindaloo and Thai red curries

You'll need the punchiest food on the planet to stand up to this meal-in-a-glass wine—but, that proviso aside, it's compelling. The smell of violets and red fruits floats from the glass—then you're into layers of intense flavour with a grippy, spicy flourish.

Stockists: *Almost nationwide* SuperValu/Centra; *and other outlets*

Château Cazal-Viel Saint-Chinian Cuvée des Fées

Languedoc, South of France
€10.49

Vintage: 2005
Grape: Mainly Syrah
Alcohol: 13%
Food matches: Versatile but needs robust flavours—meats; stews (especially with tomatoes and herbs); medium-strong cheeses

Among the raft of wines sent to Ireland by the Miquel family (Cazal-Viel in Tesco, Laurent Miquel in Dunnes Stores), this is the star. Smooth and charming but with southern vigour, it's like the marriage of a Languedoc farmer and a smart Parisienne.

Stockists: *Almost nationwide* Tesco

Château de Bayle Bordeaux ★

Bordeaux, France
€11.95

Vintage: 2005
Grape: Cabernet Sauvignon, Merlot
Alcohol: 13%
Plus point: Among 10 Best Wines for a Posh Dinner, page 49
Food matches: Duck; many red meats (especially lamb); vegetable dishes topped with cheese

A delightful red Bordeaux which teeters on the edge of the medium-bodied category—toppling into this section because it offers richness as well as silky elegance. Strikingly pure blackcurrant notes with a hint of mint make it hedonistic.

Stockists: *Mail order* www.louisalbrouze.com *Dublin* Bottleshop, Drummartin Rd; Louis Albrouze, Upper Leeson St; Mortons, Ranelagh **Galway** Mortons, Salthill **Waterford** Worldwide Wines, Waterford

Château Pique-Sègue Bergerac ★

Bergerac, South-West France
€9.99

Vintage: 2005
Grape: Merlot, Cabernet Franc, Cabernet Sauvignon
Alcohol: 13%
Plus point: Among 10 Bottles Most Likely to Impress a Wine Buff, page 118
Food matches: Duck; lamb; beef (try peppered steak); venison

I'll stick my neck out and say this wine tastes as good as many wines from nearby Bordeaux at twice the price. Plummy and mouthcoatingly rich with a firm, peppery finale, it's all about balance and harmony. It needs meat to shine, however.

Stockists: *Dublin Bennetts, Howth; Carvills, Camden St; Cellars Big Wine Warehouse, Naas Rd; Comet, Santry; Corks, Terenure; Donnybrook Fair; Drink Store, Manor St; Eurospar, Rathcoole; Gibneys, Malahide; Goose, Drumcondra; Higgins, Clonskeagh; Jus de Vine, Portmarnock; Molloys outlets; Redmonds, Ranelagh; Unwined, Swords; Vintry, Rathgar* **Galway** *Vineyard, Galway* **Kildare** *Mill Wine Cellar, Maynooth* **Meath** *Bunch of Grapes, Clonee* **Roscommon** *Dalys, Boyle* **Tipperary** *Lonergans, Clonmel* **Waterford** *Ardkeen Stores, Waterford* **Wicklow** *Hollands, Bray*

ARGENTINE BEAUTY.
TRAPICHE WINES.

Trapiche wines reveal the
extraordinary potential held in the wide
variety of Argentina's terroirs.

TRAPICHE
ARGENTINA
www.trapiche.com.ar

Domaine de Bisconte   ★
Côtes du Roussillon

Roussillon, South of France
€11.50

Vintage: 2006
Grape: Syrah, Grenache, Carignan
Alcohol: 13%
Food matches: Lamb, beef, pork or game (especially when cooked with garlic and herbs); stuffed aubergines

Here is another wine that I've kept tabs on for years—and it hasn't failed me yet. The rich damson flavours edged with liquorice are as appealing as the silky texture, while herb and black olive notes give it a terrific Mediterranean personality

Stockists: *Almost nationwide Next Door* **Clare** *Jaynes, Ennis* **Dublin** *Listons, Camden Street; On the Grapevine, Booterstown; Searsons, Monkstown* **Waterford** *Ardkeen Stores, Waterford; Garveys, Waterford*

Domaine des Coccinelles Côtes du Rhône

Southern Rhône Valley, France
€10.99

Vintage: 2006
Grape: Grenache, Syrah, Mourvèdre, Cinsault
Alcohol: 14%
Plus point: Organically grown grapes
Food matches: Lamb, beef or pork (especially when cooked with garlic and herbs); rich vegetarian dishes

Possibly (but not necessarily) because it is organic, this rich, fleshy Côtes du Rhône has an earthiness which I find attractive: it smells and tastes like a product of the soil rather than the chemistry lab. Many inexpensive wines don't! Gutsy, spicy, likeable.

Stockists: *Cork O'Donovans outlets Dublin Coach House, Ballinteer; Goose, Drumcondra; Jus de Vine, Portmarnock; McCabes, Blackrock & Foxrock; McHughs, Artane & Kilbarrack; Redmonds, Ranelagh Galway Salthill Liquor Store, Salthill Sligo Currids, Sligo Tipperary Kellers Take Home, Roscrea; Lonergans, Clonmel Waterford Worldwide Wines, Waterford Wicklow Capranis, Ashford; Hollands, Bray*

Domaine Grès Saint Vincent ★
Côtes du Rhône Villages Sinargues

Southern Rhône Valley, France
€10.99

Vintage: 2006
Grape: Grenache, Syrah
Alcohol: 14.5%
Plus point: Among 10 Best Wines for a Posh Dinner, page 49; also 10 Best Wines for Christmas, page 133
Food matches: Versatile—beef; lamb; pork; chicken; duck; vegetarian dishes. . . almost anything, spicy foods included

A little gentler than the Côtes du Rhône on the previous page, this is the kind of wine that everybody should stock up on. Not only is it stylish (that high alcohol doesn't show) but it will suit any occasion, any kind of food. Stunning for the money.

Stockists: *Almost nationwide* *Superquinn*

Domaine Lafond Roc-Épine Côtes du Rhône

Southern Rhône Valley, France
€10.99

Vintage: 2007
Grape: Grenache, Syrah
Alcohol: 13.5%
Plus point: Among 10 Best Wines for a Big Party, page 66
Food matches: Versatile—especially good with lamb; chicken; duck; vegetarian gratins or stews; also fine without food

Enticingly perfumed and impressively pure in flavour (raspberries, black cherries, black chocolate, delicate spice), this wine is a charmer. Although generously proportioned, it is also refined—not an everyday combo at this price.

Stockists: *Mail order* www.enowine.ie
Dublin *Enowine, IFSC & Monkstown* **Louth** *Callans, Dundalk; Egans, Drogheda* **Meath** *O'Dwyers, Navan*

Douglas Green The Delivery Cabernet Sauvignon-Shiraz

Western Cape, South Africa
€11.99

Vintage: 2006
Grape: Cabernet Sauvignon, Shiraz
Alcohol: 14%
Food matches: Grilled or roast meats; meat casseroles with tomatoes, garlic and herbs; rich vegetarian stews

Well crafted and confident, this intensely flavoured Cape red is so juicy and balanced that it carries off its high alcohol with aplomb. Attractive plum and blackberry notes run all the way through with a pinch of herbs to add intrigue.

Stockists: *Almost nationwide* Dunnes Stores

www.approachwines.com

Dedication, passion, expertise, local knowledge – an unrivalled combination

Approach Trade

Estampa Reserve Assemblage Cabernet Sauvignon-Carmenère-Petit Verdot

Colchagua Valley, Chile
€11.99

Vintage: 2005
Grape: Cabernet Sauvignon, Carmenère, Petit Verdot
Alcohol: 14.5%
Food matches: Lamb or beef (roast or grilled especially);
mushroom-based dishes; mature cheeses

Another tightrope act: somehow this big bruiser of a wine manages to keep its balance so that the audience remains totally engaged. Aged in barrel and bottle before release, it has enough maturity for the complex flavours to have integrated nicely.

Stockists: *Dublin* *Brackens, Glasnevin; Bradys, Shankill; Carvills, Camden St; Coach House, Ballinteer; Deveneys, Rathmines; Gibneys, Malahide; Goose, Drumcondra; Hole in the Wall, Blackhorse Ave; Jus de Vine, Portmarnock* **Wicklow** *Hollands, Bray* **Kildare** *Mill Wine Cellar, Maynooth* **Meath** *Bunch of Grapes, Clonee*

Evohé Garnacha Viñas Viejas

Aragon, North-East Spain
€11.99

Vintage: 2006
Grape: Garnacha
Alcohol: 14.5%
Plus point: Grapes from old vines
Food matches: Versatile—roasts; grills; stews (vegetarian included); meaty pizza and pasta. Herbs like thyme and rosemary will help.

With its heady aromas of fresh raspberries, cherries, herbs and spice, this is a cracking example of Garnacha in its most seductive form. There's no oak influence—just those juicy red fruit flavours with a little bit of lingering grip.

Stockists: *Clare Egans Wines, Liscannor* **Cork** *Karwig, Carrigaline* **Dublin** *64 Wine, Glasthule; Fallon & Byrne, Exchequer St; Gibneys, Malahide; Michaels Wines, Mount Merrion; Mitchell & Son, CHQ Building IFSC, Glasthule & Rathfarnham; Redmonds, Ranelagh; Sweeneys, Glasnevin; Unwined, Swords* **Kerry** *Kingdom Stores, Tralee* **Kilkenny** *Next Door, Thomastown* **Waterford** *Ardkeen Stores, Waterford* **Wicklow** *Wicklow Wine Co, Wicklow*

Finca La Celia La Consulta Malbec

Uco Valley-Mendoza, Argentina
€11.99

Vintage: 2006
Grape: Malbec
Alcohol: 13.5%
Plus point: Among 10 Bottles Most Likely to Impress a Wine Buff, page 118
Food matches: Red meats—grilled, roast, casseroled or in pies; strong (but not blue) cheeses

Christmassy spices lead the way into this intensely concentrated Malbec. Plum and blackberry flavours are matched by a meaty richness—a chewiness, almost. Even apart from the show-off tall bottle, this is posh.

Stockists: *Cork O'Donovans outlets* **Dublin** *Bin No 9, Goatstown; Donnybrook Fair, Donnybrook; McCabes, Blackrock & Foxrock; Sweeneys, Glasnevin; Thomas Deli, Foxrock* **Kerry** *Kingdom Stores, Tralee*

Finca Labarca Rioja Crianza

Rioja, North-East Spain
€9.99

Vintage: 2005
Grape: Tempranillo
Alcohol: 14%
Food matches: Lamb, pork or beef—roast, grilled or in rich stews; hearty vegetarian dishes; mature cheeses

A Rioja with a modern image—a curvy creature, sexily dressed and none the worse for having put on a bit of extra weight. Although it's quite full-on, the classic notes are there: plums, strawberries, vanilla, spice and the juice from a meat roast.

Stockists: *Almost nationwide* SuperValu/Centra

Fish Hoek

Allied Drinks Distributors Ltd
24 Parkwest Enterprise Centre, Nangor Road, Dublin 12 Tel: 01 642 9000

Finca Sophenia Altosur Malbec

Tupungato-Mendoza, Argentina
€11.50

Vintage: 2006
Grape: Malbec
Alcohol: 13.5%
Food matches: Best with meats—beef, lamb, pork (grilled or roast especially)

It's the chewy, savoury finish that makes this a meat-loving wine. But that's not to deny its fragrant, fruity charm—like an autumn compote with a pinch of spice. Layers of flavour build up impressively and ebb slowly. Great.

Stockists: *Mail order* www.jnwine.com **Cork** Parsons Wines, Carrigaline **Dublin** Canters, Fairview; Drink Store, Manor St; Goggins, Monkstown; Redmonds, Ranelagh; Sweeneys, Glasnevin **Galway** Mad About Wine, Moycullen **Waterford** Worldwide Wines, Waterford **Wicklow** Hollands, Bray

Flagstone Fish Hoek Shiraz

Western Cape, South Africa
€9.99

Vintage: 2006
Grape: Shiraz
Alcohol: 14.5%
Plus point: Screwcap; among 10 Best Wines for Spicy Foods, page 41
Food matches: Red meats (in spicy dishes, especially); rich, spicy vegetarian dishes; also good by itself on a winter night

Probably the easiest-to-spot bottle in this book, thanks to the white fish skeleton painted on the glass. The wine is big and bold, too, without being overbearing. Northern Rhône Syrah notes of tar, leather and black pepper mingle with luscious SA berry richness.

Stockists: *Almost nationwide* *Dunnes Stores; Next Door; Superquinn; SuperValu/Centra* **Cork** *O'Donovans outlets* **Dublin** *McHughs, Artane & Kilbarrack; Mitchell & Son, CHQ Building IFSC, Glasthule & Rathfarnham; Molloys outlets; Mortons, Ranelagh; Redmonds, Ranelagh; Vintry, Rathgar* **Wicklow** *Wicklow Wine Co, Wicklow*

Geoff Merrill Cabernet-Merlot

South Australia
€8.99

Vintage: 2003
Grape: Cabernet Sauvignon, Merlot
Alcohol: 14%
Plus point: Screwcap; among 10 Best Recession-Busters, page 13
Food matches: Sausages; grilled or roast lamb; roast beef or steak; nut roast; cheese and potato gratin

How Mr Merrill, one of the most flamboyant characters in Australian wine, makes a wine as understated and graceful as this is puzzling. How he manages it at the price is utterly baffling. It's rich but not heavy or flashy—and always mature on release.

Stockists: *Dublin* *Bennetts, Howth; Bin No 9, Goatstown; Comet, Santry; Donnybrook Fair, Donnybrook; Goose, Drumcondra; Higgins, Clonskeagh; Jus de Vine, Portmarnock; Londis, Malahide; Molloys outlets; O'Neills, SC Rd; Red Island, Skerries; Spar, Ballycullen; Unwined, Swords*
Kildare *Mill Wine Cellar, Maynooth **Meath** Next Door, Enfield*
Roscommon *Dalys, Boyle **Wicklow** Hollands, Bray*

Goats Do Roam

Western Cape, South Africa
€10.99–€11.50

Vintage: 2006
Grape: Shiraz, Pinotage, Cinsault, Mourvèdre, Grenache, Carignan
Alcohol: 14.5%
Plus point: Screwcap
Food matches: Needs strong flavours—beef or pork, barbecued or in a rich stew; Mediterranean-style vegetable dishes

Maverick winemaker Charles Back loves poking fun at the French with his cheekily-named Côtes du Rhône take-off. (He keeps goats at the winery, so can plead innocence.) Brash, uncomplicated, fiery… a fun wine with plenty to say for itself.

Stockists: *Almost nationwide* O'Briens **Dublin** *Flanagans, Harolds Cross; Jus de Vine, Portmarnock; Marthas Vineyard, Rathfarnham* **Kerry** *Centra, Killorgan* **Limerick** *Fine Wines, Limerick* **Meath** *Centra, Navan* **Wicklow** *Next Door, Blessington*

Hout Bay Shiraz

Western Cape, South Africa
€10.95–€11.50

Vintage: 2007
Grape: Shiraz
Alcohol: 14%
Plus point: Screwcap
Food matches: Robust flavours—spicy sausages; spare ribs; barbecued meats; medium-spicy dishes; rich vegetable stews; also fine by itself

Some New World Shiraz can be on the jammy side—but not this one. The topnotes belong to fresh, juicy fruits—black cherries, blackberries, damsons. Underneath lies a layer of fine tannins with a touch of minerality. Very smart indeed.

Stockists: *Cork O'Donovans outlets* **Dublin** *Bin No. 9, Goatstown; Donnybrook Fair, Donnybrook; McCabes, Blackrock & Foxrock; Sweeneys, Glasnevin; Thomas Deli, Foxrock* **Kerry** *Kingdom Stores, Tralee*

La Ferme du Mont 'Le Ponnant' Côtes du Rhône Villages

Southern Rhône Valley, France
€10.99–€11.99

Vintage: 2006
Grape: Grenache, Syrah
Alcohol: 14.5%
Plus point: Among 10 Best Wines for Christmas, page 133
Food matches: Versatile—beef; lamb; pork; chicken; duck; many vegetarian dishes. . . almost anything, spicy foods included

If wines had visual expressions, this one would be smiling. Smooth, even and generously flavoured with the usual Southern Rhône amalgam of dark fruits and a hint of tar, it's straightforward and easy-going—easy to drink, easy to match.

Stockists: *Dublin* Bennetts, Howth; Corkscrew, Chatham St; Deveneys, Dundrum; Fresh, Grand Canal, Northern Cross & Smithfield; Jus de Vine, Portmarnock; Kellys, Clontarf; Nolans, Clontarf; Redmonds, Ranelagh; Sheils, Dorset St; Strand, Fairview; Sweeneys, Glasnevin; Thomas Martin, Fairview; Thomas Deli, Foxrock; Wilde & Green, Milltown **Kildare** Swans on the Green, Naas **Tipperary** Eldons, Clonmel **Wicklow** Wicklow Arms, Delgany

Le Petit Jaboulet Syrah Vin de Pays

South of France
€11.99

Vintage: 2006
Grape: Syrah
Alcohol: 13.5%
Food matches: Very versatile—will suit poultry, meats and rich vegetarian dishes (with Mediterranean flavours especially)

Long established in the Northern Rhône, the house of Jaboulet spreads its wings by making an all-Syrah wine with grapes from further south. Very Mediterranean in style it is, too, with overtones of provencal herbs floating over ripe, juicy red fruits.

Stockists: *Dublin* *Bennetts, Howth; Bin No. 9, Goatstown; Boozebusters outlets; Cellars Big Wine Warehouse, Naas Rd; Deveneys, Dundrum; Donnybrook Fair, Donnybrook; Jus de Vine, Portmarnock; Lilac Wines, Fairview; McCabes, Blackrock & Foxrock; McHughs, Artane & Kilbarrack* **Galway** *Harvest outlets* **Kildare** *Next Door, Clane* **Laois** *Egans, Portlaoise* **Louth** *Callans, Dundalk* **Offaly** *Lynchs Bottleshop, Tullamore* **Tipperary** *Eldons, Clonmel; Lonergans, Clonmel* **Waterford** *Ardkeen Stores, Waterford; Worldwide Wines, Waterford* **Wexford** *Greenacres, Wexford* **Wicklow** *Hollands, Bray*

MAN Vintners Shiraz

Coastal Region, South Africa
€10.99–€11.50

Vintage: 2006
Grape: Shiraz
Alcohol: 14%
Plus point: Screwcap
Food matches: Versatile—most meats; poultry; many vegetable, cheese and egg-based dishes; also fine without food

Created by three winemakers with talent (and romance—M, A & N are the initials of their wives' names), this is a sleek, modern Shiraz. Although the flavours are agreeably assertive, it's smooth as satin—so food is optional.

Stockists: *Dublin Bennetts, Howth; Cellars Big Wine Warehouse, Naas Rd; Jus de Vine, Portmarnock; Lilac Wines, Fairview; Liz Delaneys, Coolock; Marthas Vineyard, Rathfarnham; McCabes, Blackrock & Foxrock; McHughs, Artane & Kilbarrack* **Galway** *Harvest outlets* **Laois** *Egans, Portlaoise* **Louth** *Callans, Dundalk; Shermans Off-Licence, Dunleer* **Offaly** *Lynchs Bottleshop, Tullamore* **Tipperary** *Eldons, Clonmel; Lonergans, Clonmel* **Waterford** *Ardkeen Stores, Waterford; Worldwide Wines, Waterford* **Wexford** *Greenacres, Wexford* **Wicklow** *Hollands, Bray*

Marks & Spencer Ripasso Valpolicella Classico

Veneto, North-East Italy
€10.99

Vintage: 2006
Grape: Corvina, Rondinella, Molinara
Alcohol: 13.5%
Food matches: Beef—roast or casseroled (especially with mushrooms); steak in red wine sauce; venison; parmesan cheese; or by itself as a nightcap

No doubt our climate makes us crave ultra-rich reds—so ripasso styles are a big hit in Ireland. Made by adding semi-dried grapes into the fermentation, most are pricey—which makes this smooth, luscious, cherry-liqueur-tinged beauty a great find.

Stockists: *Almost nationwide* Marks & Spencer

Montesierra Tempranillo-Cabernet

Somontano, North-East Spain
€9.50

Vintage: 2007
Grape: Tempranillo, Cabernet Sauvignon, Moristel
Alcohol: 13%
Food matches: Versatile—most meats; flavoursome vegetarian dishes; cheese-based dishes

The rise of the New Spain—areas beyond well-known Rioja and Ribera del Duero—is largely based on the production of a panoply of affordable, appetising wines like this. Plump fruitiness is matched by peppery punch.

Stockists: *Mail order* www.spanishwines.ie

www.approachwines.com

Dedication, passion, expertise, local knowledge – an unrivalled combination

Approach Trade

Norte Chico Merlot

Central Valley, Chile
€9.99–€10.50

Vintage: 2007
Grape: Merlot
Alcohol: 13%
Plus point: Screwcap
Food matches: Versatile—suits meats of most kinds; flavoursome vegetable-based dishes; cheese-based dishes; nut roast

Amongst scads of Chilean Merlots sampled for this book, this is one that stands out for its sheer oomph. It delivers heaps of flavour—fresh red fruits, a touch of spice, earthy and mineral nuances—along with vigour and grip.

Stockists: *Mail order* www.jnwine.com

Olivier Cuilleras Vin de Pays

Comté de Grignan, Southern Rhône Valley, France
€9.95

Vintage: 2006
Grape: Grenache, Syrah
Alcohol: 13.5%
Food matches: Meats, grilled, roast or casseroled; hearty vegetable
stews; pasta with a rich sauce; lentil-based dishes

From a sixth-generation grape grower,
here's a well-turned-out cousin of Côtes
du Rhône at a succulent price. As well as
opulent, dark fruit flavours there are hints
of smoke and tar, pepper and spice in a
nice, fleshy body.

Stockists: *Mail order* www.louisalbrouze.com
Dublin Bottleshop, Drummartin Rd; Louis Albrouze,
Upper Leeson St; Mortons, Ranelagh
Galway Mortons, Salthill **Waterford** Worldwide
Wines, Waterford

Paulo Laureano Clássico Vinho Regional

Alentejo, Portugal
€11.95

Vintage: 2006
Grape: Trincadeira, Aragonés
Alcohol: 13.5%
Food matches: Richly flavoured pork, beef or vegetable stews; spicy sausages; stuffed mushrooms

There's a warm, enveloping aspect to this mouthcoating Portuguese red—so drinking it is rather like snuggling into a big, soft, woolly jumper. Rich damson flavours are complemented by earthy tones and a hint of liquorice. Gutsy but polished.

Stockists: *Mail order* www.mitchellandson.com
Dublin *Mitchell & Son, CHQ Building IFSC, Glasthule & Rathfarnham*

Poggio del Sasso Sangiovese di Toscana ★

Tuscany, Central Italy
€11.99

Vintage: 2006
Grape: Sangiovese
Alcohol: 13%
Plus point: Screwcap; among 10 Best Wines for a Posh Dinner, page 49
Food matches: Beef; lamb; pork; duck; robust vegetarian dishes; garlic, herbs and/or a tomato sauce will help the match

So aromatic is this smoky, earthy, cherry-and-chocolate-rich wine that you imagine a mouthful or two may be totally overwhelming. Not so. Although flavour-packed and meaty, it is refreshingly juicy. Perfectly balanced, in other words— and alluring.

Stockists: *Mail order wineonline.ie **Dublin** 64 Wine, Glasthule; Bin No 9, Goatstown; Donnybrook Fair, Donnybrook; Drink Store, Manor St; Enowine, IFSC & Monkstown; Fallon & Byrne, Exchequer St; Hole in the Wall, Blackhorse Ave; Lilac Wines, Fairview; Red Island Wines, Skerries **Kilkenny** Le Caveau, Kilkenny*

Principe de Viana Navarra Tempranillo ★

Navarra, North-East Spain
€11.99

Vintage: 2007
Grape: Tempranillo
Alcohol: 13.5%
Food matches: Lamb in any shape or form (including liver); pork chops; chargrilled duck breasts; cheese-topped vegetable gratins

From a frontline Navarra producer (whose rosé is also in this book, see page 57), this terrific Tempranillo bursts into life at first sip. Rich damson and blackberry flavours are perked up by black pepper and liquorice thrust.

Stockists: ***Cork*** *O'Donovans outlets* **Dublin** *Bin No. 9, Goatstown; Donnybrook Fair, Donnybrook; Gibneys, Malahide; McCabes, Blackrock & Foxrock; Sweeneys, Glasnevin; Thomas Deli, Foxrock; Whelans, Wexford St* **Kerry** *Kingdom Stores, Tralee*

Rocca Ventosa Montepulciano d'Abruzzo

Montepulciano d'Abruzzo, Central Italy
€11.99

Vintage: 2006
Grape: Montepulciano
Alcohol: 12.5%
Food matches: Lamb, pork, beef or Mediterranean vegetables—especially when roast with rosemary or thyme

Cherryish and herbal, brooding and complex, polished and earthy, velvety and mouthcoating... this quintessential Italian has everything you could hope for and more. It's a much richer wine than its 12.5% alcohol suggests and oh, so tasty.

Stockists: *Cork* O'Donovans outlets **Dublin** Bin No. 9, Goatstown; Donnybrook Fair, Donnybrook; McCabes, Blackrock & Foxrock; Sweeneys, Glasnevin; Thomas Deli, Foxrock **Kerry** Kingdom Stores, Tralee

San Pedro Cabernet Sauvignon Reserva

Lontué Valley, Chile
€9.99

Vintage: 2005
Grape: Cabernet Sauvignon
Alcohol: 14.5%
Food matches: Best with meat—roast beef or steak; grilled or roast lamb; sausages

For less than a tenner this wine offers a lot. Although it's big and brawny with a fleshy texture and powerful concentration, the flavours are subtle and harmonious—so you aren't left with the feeling that it's OTT. Do treat it to meat, though.

Stockists: *Almost nationwide* Dunnes Stores

Santa Helena Selección Cabernet Sauvignon Reserva

Colchagua Valley, Chile
€9.99

Vintage: 2005
Grape: Cabernet Sauvignon
Alcohol: 14%
Food matches: Beef; lamb; pork; most spicy meat dishes; hearty vegetable or cheese-based dishes

Compared to the Chilean Cab on the previous page, this one is less meaty and more voluptuous. Very smooth, almost creamy, with rich overtones of cassis liqueur, dark chocolate and spice, it's quite a versatile wine with strikingly pure flavours.

Stockists: *Almost nationwide* Eurospar; Mace; SPAR

Santa Julia Malbec

Mendoza, Argentina
€9.99

Vintage: 2006
Grape: Malbec
Alcohol: 13.5%
Food matches: Grilled or roast meats of all kinds (lamb is especially good); chilli con carne; pasta with meat sauce; toasted cheese sandwiches

I admire the energetic, questing Zuccardi family behind Santa Julia. Year after year they manage to turn Argentina's star red grape into a consistently pleasing wine. Not too luscious (as Malbec can sometimes be): the endnote is firm and dry.

Stockists: *Almost nationwide* Dunnes Stores; *SuperValu/Centra* **Galway** Harvest outlets **Laois** *Portlaoise Wine Vault, Portlaoise*

T'Air d'Oc Syrah Vin de Pays d'Oc ★

Languedoc, South of France
€10.95

Vintage: 2006
Grape: Syrah
Alcohol: 13%
Plus point: Screwcap; among 10 Best Wines for a Big Party, page 66
Food matches: Many medium-weight dishes—grilled chicken; cold meats; gammon steaks; quiche lorraine; vegetable frittata; also fine without food

No wonder the Syrah bandwagon is hurtling along with wines like this to propel it forward. From dynamic Domaine Gayda, it's all about fresh, fruity charm—as seductively perfumed as Beaujolais but with more body and depth. Just yummy.

Stockists: *Mail order* www.jnwine.com **Wicklow** *Roundwood Food & Wine, Roundwood*

10 bottles most likely to impress a wine buff

Aperitif

- Marks & Spencer Manzanilla Sherry
  €7.49 (page 128)

White

- Alain Brumont Gros Manseng-Sauvignon Blanc Vin de Pays des Côtes de Gascogne
  €11.35 (page 2)
- Dolle Grüner Veltliner Strassertal
  €9.99 (page 36)
- Schloss Schörnborn Riesling Trocken
  €11.49 (page 24)
- Tahbilk Nagambie Lakes Marsanne
  €11.99 (page 44)

Rosé

- Petit Bourgeois Rosé de Pinot Noir, Vin de Pays du Val de Loire
  €11.99 (page 56)

Red

- Chateau Pique-Sègue Bergerac
  €9.99 (page 7)
- Bestué de Otto Bestué Somontano Finca Rableros
  €9.99 (page 80)
- Finca La Celia La Consulta Malbec
  €11.99 (page 96)
- Yering Station Little Yering Pinot Noir
  €11.99 (page 77)

Tesco Argentina Malbec Reserve

Mendoza, Argentina
€5.99

Vintage: 2007
Grape: Malbec
Alcohol: 13%
Plus point: Screwcap; among 10 Best Recession-Busters, page 13
Food matches: Hamburgers; beef tacos or burritos; pasta with meat sauce; pepperoni pizza; lentil rissoles; cheese-based dishes

Let's be honest: not the very best wine in this book. But it is the cheapest by far—and still good enough to pass the taste test. Plummy, brambly flavours are mixed with a dollop of spice and a touch of savoury firmness.

Stockists: *Almost nationwide* Tesco

Allied Drinks Distributors Ltd
24 Parkwest Enterprise Centre, Nangor Road, Dublin 12
Tel: 01 642 9000

ERRAZURIZ

Tesco Finest Vacqueyras

Southern Rhône Valley, France
€11.99

Vintage: 2006
Grape: Grenache, Syrah, Mourvèdre
Alcohol: 13.5%
Food matches: Lamb, pork or beef—grilled or roast; rich meat or vegetable casseroles; moussaka; venison; strong cheeses

If the Southern Rhône is over-represented in this book, it's because its rich, round, warming reds are so appealing—and so food-flexible. This one works its magic with a pillow of ripe, juicy berry fruits on a firm bed of spicy richness.

Stockists: *Almost nationwide* Tesco

Intensity captured.

AUSTRALIAN
CRAFTSMANSHIP
SINCE 1828

WYNDHAM
ESTATE
Since 1828

BIN
555

SHIRAZ

*More than 170 years ago, George Wyndham
planted Australia's first commercial Shiraz
vineyard and began handcrafting intensely
flavoured wines. Today, BIN 555 is the
definitive Australian Shiraz, layered with rich
generous plum and berry flavours.*

SOUTH EASTERN AUSTRALIA

Where Australian Shiraz began.

Enjoy WYNDHAM ESTATE Sensibly

Visit drinkaware.ie

The Wolftrap Syrah-Mourvèdre-Viognier

Western Cape, South Africa
€8.99

Vintage: 2006
Grape: Syrah, Mourvèdre, Viognier
Alcohol: 14%
Plus point: Screwcap; among 10 Best Recession-Busters, page 13
Food matches: Big, meaty, smoky flavours—barbecued meats; spicy bean and chorizo stew; chargrilled aubergines; strong cheeses

From Rhône-obsessed winemaker Marc Kent of Boekenhoutskloof comes the wine equivalent of an All-Black. This is a massive red—powerful and brooding with dense, spicy fruit and smoky allure. A barbecue humdinger or enjoy it in winter by the fire.

Stockists: *Almost nationwide* Superquinn

Vega del Castillo Garnacha Cepas Viejas

Navarra, North-East Spain
€9.99

Vintage: 2005
Grape: Garnacha
Alcohol: 13%
Plus point: Grapes from old vines
Food matches: Rustic pâtés; braised lamb shanks; spicy lamb dishes; duck; lentil-based dishes

This wine delivers all the richness you might hope for in a wine made from the extra-flavoursome grapes of 60-year-old vines. Raspberry and violet notes make it immediately enticing; then comes a gentle but persistent tannic squeeze.

Stockists: *Dublin Bradys, Bakers Corner & Shankill; Carvills, Camden Street; Cellars Big Wine Warehouse, Naas Rd; Coach House, Ballinteer; Deveneys, Rathmines; Walsh Wines, Dun Laoghaire*

Wakefield Estate Cabernet Sauvignon

Clare Valley, South Australia
€11.99

Vintage: 2006
Grape: Cabernet Sauvignon
Alcohol: 14.5%
Plus point: Screwcap
Food matches: Lamb or beef—roast, grilled, casseroled with herbs
or in spicy dishes; hearty vegetable or cheese-based dishes

One of the first wines I recommended as
a wine writer, back in 1995—and it's still a
goody. Smooth blackcurrant richness is
lifted by a fresh, juicy tang and a nice little
dash of liquorice and thyme—slowly giving
way to a firm, dry finale.

Stockists: *Almost nationwide Dunnes Stores;
O'Briens; SuperValu/Centra **Donegal** Next Door,
Killybegs **Dublin** Bennetts, Howth; Coach House,
Ballinteer; Coolers, Applewood; Jus de Vine,
Portmarnock **Galway** Harvest outlets; Joyces, Galway
& Headford **Meath** Bunch of Grapes, Clonee
Roscommon Clarks, Boyle **Waterford** Ardkeen
Stores, Waterford*

SHERRIES

Berrys' Fino Sherry

Jerez, Spain
€11.95

Vintage: Non-vintage
Grape: Palomino Fino
Alcohol: 15.5%
Food matches: Aperitif with almonds, olives, tapas; Spanish ham, chorizo sausage and other smoky flavours

Made for Berrys by the respected Lustau bodega, this fino is fuller in flavour than many with a touch of spice and a warm, savoury richness that makes me think of marmite on toast. Try it with quite robust food flavours—even if only in nibbles.

Stockists: *Mail order* www.bbr.ie **Dublin** Berry Bros & Rudd, Harry St

Marks & Spencer Dry Fino Sherry ★

Jerez, Spain
€7.49

Vintage: Non-vintage
Grape: Palomino Fino
Alcohol: 15%
Plus point: Screwcap; among 10 Best Recession-Busters, see page 13
Food matches: Aperitif with almonds, olives, prawns, anchovies, other tapas; Spanish ham; fish and chips

Smooth and stylish, this is one of the best bargains I have ever (ever!) come across. A little rounder and nuttier than the equally tasty manzanilla on the next page, it's versatile and appealing enough to deserve a place in every fridge.

Stockists: ***Almost nationwide*** *Marks & Spencer*

Marks & Spencer Manzanilla Sherry

Jerez, Spain
€7.49

Vintage: Non-vintage
Grape: Palomino Fino
Alcohol: 15%
Plus point: Screwcap; among 10 Bottles Most Likely to Impress a Wine Buff, page 118
Food matches: Aperitif with almonds, olives, tapas; light fish; seafood

With sherry back in fashion the spotlight is on manzanilla, the lightest, trendiest sherry style. Matured in bodegas aired by sea breezes, it has a bracing, salty tang—here amplified by lemon, almond and green olive flavours. Very appetising.

Stockists: *Almost nationwide Marks & Spencer*

SPARKLING
WINES

Bortolotti d'Arcàne Prosecco di Valdobbiadene Frizzante

Veneto, North-East Italy
€14.99

Vintage: Non-vintage
Grape: Prosecco
Alcohol: 11%
Food matches: Aperitif (especially with olives and almonds); mixed antipasti or other light first courses

Even if the aromas of this gently fizzy prosecco don't entirely win you over, its refined flavours and delicious, lingering aftertaste surely will. Unlike many proseccos, it has no harsh bite in the finish—just moreish appeal.

Stockists: *Mail order* www.enowine.ie
Dublin *Enowine, IFSC & Monkstown* **Louth** *Callans, Dundalk; Egans, Drogheda* **Meath** *O'Dwyers, Navan*

Castillo Perelada Cava Brut Reserva

Catalunya, North-East Spain
€13.99

Vintage: Non-vintage
Grape: Parellada, Macabeo, Xarel-lo
Alcohol: 11.5%
Food matches: Aperitif; tapas; light Chinese or Indian starters

Spain's popular fizz suffers from an image problem—partly because too many cavas have strong vegetal aromas and flavours which are downright offputting. This one doesn't. With soft pear, lemon and honey notes, it's very quaffable indeed.

Stockists: *Dublin Bennetts, Howth; Bin No 9, Goatstown; Carvills, Camden St; Cellars Big Wine Warehouse, Naas Rd; Deveneys, Dundrum & Rathmines; Donnybrook Fair; Drink Store, Manor St; Eurospar, Rathcoole; Gibneys, Malahide; Goose, Drumcondra; Higgins, Clonskeagh; Jus de Vine, Portmarnock; Mortons, Ranelagh; Molloys outlets; On the Grapevine, Booterstown & Dalkey; Red Island, Skerries; Redmonds, Ranelagh; SuperValu/Centra, Raheny; Unwined, Swords **Galway** Vineyard, Galway **Kildare** Mill Wine Cellar, Maynooth **Meath** Coolers, Clonee; Next Door, Enfield **Roscommon** Dalys, Boyle **Tipperary** Lonergans, Clonmel **Waterford** Ardkeen Stores, Waterford **Wicklow** Wicklow Arms, Delgany*

Codorníu Cava Reserva Raventos

Catalunya, North-East Spain
€14.99

Vintage: Non-vintage
Grape: Parellada, Macabeo, Xarel-lo, Chardonnay
Alcohol: 11.5%
Plus point: Among 10 Best Wines for Christmas, page 133
Food matches: Aperitif (especially with olives, almonds, cheese snacks or tapas); excellent brunch partner with eggs or smoked salmon

With Chardonnay added into the traditional blend for extra smoothness and more depth of fruity flavour, this is a Jeremy Clarkson of a cava. Big, bold, assured. . . and irresistibly refreshing. An invigorating wake-up bubbly—great for a weekend brunch.

Stockists: *Almost nationwide Dunnes Stores; O'Briens; SuperValu/Centra; and many independent off-licences*

10 best wines for Christmas

Sparkling aperitifs

- **Codorníu Cava Reserva Raventos**
  €14.99 (page 132) *would also be excellent with a first course of smoked salmon*

- **Marks & Spencer Prosecco Raboso Rosé Spumante Brut**
  €12.49 (page 137) *pretty with a few frozen cranberries in the bottom of the glass*

Whites for oysters

- **Flying Kiwi Marlborough Sauvignon Blanc**
  €9.99 (page 11)

- **Tesco Tingleup Vineyard Riesling**
  €10.99 (page 27)

Whites for smoked salmon

- **Louis Latour Ardèche Chardonnay**
  €10.99–€11.50 (page 38)

- **Simone Joseph Chardonnay Vin de Pays**
  €11.95 (page 43)

Reds for turkey

- **Domaine Grès Saint Vincent Côtes du Rhône Villages Sinargues**
  €10.99 (page 91)

- **La Ferme du Mont Côtes du Rhône Villages Le Ponnant**
  €10.99–€11.99 (page 103)

- **Secano Estate Leyda Valley Pinot Noir**
  €10.99 (page 74)

Christmas pudding wine

- **Moscato d'Asti Ca'Bianca**
  €11.99 (page 139)

Guerrieri-Rizzardi Prosecco Vino Spumante Extra Dry ★

Veneto, North-East Italy
€14.99

Vintage: Non-vintage
Grape: Prosecco
Alcohol: 11%
Plus point: Among 10 Best Wines for a Posh Dinner, page 49
Food matches: Aperitif (especially with olives and almonds); mixed antipasti or other light first courses

From an ace producer (whose scrumptious rosé is on page 54), this elegant fizz builds the bracing freshness associated with good prosecco into a soft pillow of ripe pear-like fruit. The finish is just off-dry. Delicious.

Stockists: *Almost nationwide* O'Briens

Jacob's Creek Chardonnay-Pinot Noir Brut Cuvée

South Eastern Australia
€13.99

Vintage: Non-vintage
Grape: Chardonnay, Pinot Noir
Alcohol: 11.5%
Plus point: Also available in packs of 3 x 200ml bottles
Food matches: Aperitif; light first courses (Chinese, Thai, Indian included); sushi; oysters; cheese soufflés or dips

Probably the most versatile sparkling wine in this book—and very well made, as befits one of Australia's most reliable big brands. While it's crisp enough to perk up the tastebuds, the appley aromas and aftertaste are soft and gentle.

Stockists: *Almost nationwide* *Dunnes Stores; O'Briens; Superquinn; SuperValu/Centra; Tesco; and many independent off-licences countrywide* ***Dublin*** *Molloys outlets*

Jacob's Creek Sparkling Rosé Dry Cuvée

South Eastern Australia
€13.99

Vintage: Non-vintage
Grape: Chardonnay, Pinot Noir
Alcohol: 11.5%
Plus point: Among 10 Best Wines for Spicy Foods, page 41
Food matches: Aperitif; light first courses (mild-to-medium-spicy Chinese, Thai, Indian included); salmon; cold meats; red berry or chocolate desserts

If you are at all influenced by fashion (sparkling wines and rosés are on a roll, see page xi), take note of this tasty and versatile pink sparkler. A little richer than the JC fizz on the previous page, it can stand up to quite bold food flavours.

Stockists: *Almost nationwide Dunnes Stores; O'Briens; Superquinn; SuperValu/Centra; Tesco; and many independent off-licences countrywide **Dublin** Molloys outlets*

Marks & Spencer Prosecco Raboso Rosé Spumante Brut ★

Veneto, North-East Italy
€12.49

Vintage: Non-vintage
Grape: Prosecco, Raboso
Alcohol: 11%
Plus point: Among 10 Best Wines for a Big Party, page 66; also 10 Best Wines for Christmas, page 133
Food matches: Aperitif; light prawn or crab starters; mixed antipasti; tomato salad with mozzarella cheese; fresh strawberries

As pure pink prosecco is impossible, here is the next best thing: prosecco tinged pale salmon pink by the addition of a drop of the local red wine Raboso. It looks and tastes divine, with soft pear and cherry tones leading into a nice, crisp finish. Superb value.

Stockists: *Almost nationwide* *Marks & Spencer*

Marks & Spencer Vintage Cava Brut

Catalunya, North-East Spain
€12.99

Vintage: 2005
Grape: Parellada, Macabeo, Xarel-lo
Alcohol: 11.5%
Food matches: Aperitif (especially with olives, almonds, cheese snacks or tapas); excellent brunch partner with eggs and smoked salmon

Another wine that I have enjoyed for years—and I still think its quality unrivalled by any other cava at the price. Longer than average ageing on the yeast lees gives its fresh apple and lemon flavours a lovely touch of yeasty, biscuity richness.

Stockists: *Almost nationwide* Marks & Spencer

Moscato d'Asti Ca'Bianca

Piedmont, North-West Italy
€12.99

Vintage: 2007
Grape: Moscato Bianco
Alcohol: 5%
Plus point: Very low alcohol; among 10 Best Wines for Christmas, page 133
Food matches: Many light desserts—meringues; ice cream; lemon soufflé or lemon tart; pavlova; also Christmas pudding

A light, frothy fizz with a touch of sweetness can end a meal deliciously—and, in the case of Moscato d'Asti, without alcoholic overkill. Tasting of muscatel grapes and honey yet not too sweet, this is a dainty beauty.

Stockists: *Clare* *Jordans Mace, Lisdoonvara* ***Dublin*** *Corkscrew, Chatham St* ***Kildare*** *O'Rourkes, Newbridge* ***Meath*** *Dew Drop, Athboy; Next Door, Enfield* ***Waterford*** *Wine Vaults, Lismore*

Prosecco Lunetta Brut

Veneto, North-East Italy
€13.49

Vintage: Non-vintage
Grape: Prosecco
Alcohol: 11.5%
Food matches: Aperitif; many light first courses including mixed antipasti; light Chinese dishes

People who dislike the bitter almond aftertaste that is part and parcel of many proseccos will enjoy this soft, slightly peachy version from major Italian wine company Cavit. Fruity and harmonious, it aims at the popular vote. And wins!

Stockists: *Almost nationwide* Superquinn

WHERE
TO BUY
THE
WINES

The wines listed are all available either by mail order, in nationwide chains, and/or from a number of independent outlets. However, some of the more widely distributed wines are available in so many outlets it is not possible to list them all.

ALMOST NATIONWIDE

Dunnes Stores
Elegant, medium-bodied red
Antinori Santa Cristina Toscana 61
Chivite Gran Feudo Navarra Crianza 63
Montana East Coast Merlot-Cabernet Sauvignon 71
Light & refreshing white
Inycon Estate Fiano Sicilia 14
Mitchelton Blackwood Park Riesling 19
Montana East Coast Unoaked Chardonnay 20
The Beach House Sauvignon Blanc-Semillon 28
Tramoya Rueda Verdejo 29
More full-bodied white
Mitchelton Thomas Mitchell Marsanne 40
Rich full-bodied red
Bestué de Otto Bestué Somontano Finca Rableros 80
Douglas Green The Delivery Cabernet Sauvignon-Shiraz 93
Flagstone Fish Hoek Shiraz 99
San Pedro Cabernet Sauvignon Reserva 114
Santa Julia Malbec 116

Wakefield Estate Cabernet Sauvignon 124
Rosé
Chivite Gran Feudo Navarra Rosado 50
Errazuriz Estate Cabernet Sauvignon Rosé 53
Torres de Casta Rosada 58
Sparkling
Codorníu Cava Reserva Raventos 132
Jacob's Creek Chardonnay-Pinot Noir Brut Cuvée 135
Jacob's Creek Sparkling Rosé Dry Cuvée 136

Eurospar
Elegant, medium-bodied red
Flying Kiwi South Island Pinot Noir 67
Light & refreshing white
Flying Kiwi Marlborough Sauvignon Blanc 11
Kiwi Cuvée Sauvignon Blanc Vin de Pays du Val de Loire 15
Rich full-bodied red
Santa Helena Selección Cabernet Sauvignon Reserva 115

Lidl
Light & refreshing white
Chablis Thomas de Ribens 4

Londis
Elegant, medium-bodied red
Cono Sur Pinot Noir 64
Rosé
Miguel Torres Santa Digna
    Cabernet Sauvignon Rosé
    Reserve 55

Mace
Elegant, medium-bodied red
Flying Kiwi South Island Pinot
    Noir 67
Light & refreshing white
Flying Kiwi Marlborough
    Sauvignon Blanc 11
Kiwi Cuvée Sauvignon Blanc Vin
    de Pays du Val de Loire 15
Rich full-bodied red
Santa Helena Selección Cabernet
    Sauvignon Reserva 115

Marks & Spencer
Elegant, medium-bodied red
Marks & Spencer Bourgogne
    Pinot Noir 'Les Senteurs' 68
Marks & Spencer Mâcon Rouge
    69
Secano Estate Pinot Noir 74
Light & refreshing white
La Basca Verdejo 16

Marks & Spencer Mâcon-Villages
    18
More full-bodied white
Marks & Spencer Langhe Arneis
    39
Rich full-bodied red
Marks & Spencer Ripasso
    Valpolicella Classico 106
Sherry
Marks & Spencer Dry Fino
    Sherry 127
Marks & Spencer Manzanilla
    Sherry 128
Sparkling
Marks & Spencer Prosecco
    Raboso Rosé 137
Marks & Spencer Vintage Cava
    Brut 138

Next Door
Elegant, medium-bodied red
Chivite Gran Feudo Navarra
    Crianza 63
Corinto Merlot 65
Rich full-bodied red
Botalcura Syrah-Malbec Reserva
    El Delirio 82
Domaine de Bisconte Côtes du
    Roussillon 89
Flagstone Fish Hoek Shiraz 99
Rosé
Chivite Gran Feudo Navarra
    Rosado 50

143

Errazuriz Estate Cabernet
Sauvignon Rosé 53
Miguel Torres Santa Digna
Cabernet Sauvignon Rosé
Reserve 55
Torres de Casta Rosada 58

O'Briens
Elegant, medium-bodied red
Antinori Santa Cristina Toscana
61
Chivite Gran Feudo Navarra
Crianza 63
Cono Sur Pinot Noir 64
Montana East Coast Merlot-
Cabernet Sauvignon 71
Raimat Abadia Crianza 72
Light & refreshing white
Château de la Breteche
Muscadet Sèvre et Maine Sur
Lie 5
Dourthe No 1 Bordeaux
Sauvignon Blanc 10
Gavi La Battistina 12
Petit Bourgeois Sauvignon Blanc
Vin de Pays du Val de Loire 23
Schloss Schönborn Riesling
Trocken 24
Rich full-bodied red
Altano Douro 79
Bodega Norton Barrel Select
Malbec 81
Goats Do Roam 101

Wakefield Estate Cabernet
Sauvignon 124
Rosé
Chivite Gran Feudo Navarra
Rosado 50
Guerrieri-Rizzardi Rosa Rosae
Rosato 54
Petit Bourgeois Rosé de Pinot
Noir Vin de Pays 56
Sparkling
Codorníu Cava Reserva Raventos
132
Guerrieri-Rizzardi Prosecco Vino
Spumante Extra Dry 134
Jacob's Creek Chardonnay-Pinot
Noir Brut Cuvée 135
Jacob's Creek Sparkling Rosé Dry
Cuvée 136

Spar
Elegant, medium-bodied red
Flying Kiwi South Island Pinot
Noir 67
Light & refreshing white
Flying Kiwi Marlborough
Sauvignon Blanc 11
Kiwi Cuvée Sauvignon Blanc Vin
de Pays du Val de Loire 15
Rich full-bodied red
Santa Helena Selección Cabernet
Sauvignon Reserva 115

Superquinn
Elegant, medium-bodied red
Agustinos Pinot Noir Reserva 60

Chivite Gran Feudo Navarra
Crianza 63

Montana East Coast Merlot-
Cabernet Sauvignon 71

Light & refreshing white
Montana East Coast Unoaked
Chardonnay 20

Vansha Sauvignon Blanc 30

Viña Mar de Casablanca
Sauvignon Blanc Reserva 31

More full-bodied white
Dolle Grüner Veltliner Strassertal
36

Rich full-bodied red
Domaine Grès Saint Vincent
Côtes du Rhône Villages
Sinargues 91

Flagstone Fish Hoek Shiraz 99

The Wolftrap Syrah-Mourvèdre-
Viognier 122

Rosé
Chivite Gran Feudo Navarra
Rosado 50

Domaine Bégude Pinot Rosé Vin
de Pays d'Oc 51

Errazuriz Estate Cabernet
Sauvignon Rosé 53

Torres de Casta Rosada 58

Sparkling
Jacob's Creek Chardonnay-Pinot
Noir Brut Cuvée 135

Jacob's Creek Sparkling Rosé Dry
Cuvée 136

Prosecco Lunetta Brut 140

SuperValu/Centra
Elegant, medium-bodied red
Antinori Santa Cristina Toscana
61

Cono Sur Pinot Noir 64

Montana East Coast Merlot-
Cabernet Sauvignon 71

Tyrrell's Old Winery Pinot Noir
76

Light & refreshing white
Montana East Coast Unoaked
Chardonnay 20

Rich full-bodied red
Carmen Syrah 83

Finca Labarca Rioja Crianza 97

Flagstone Fish Hoek Shiraz 99

Santa Julia Malbec 116

Wakefield Estate Cabernet
Sauvignon 124

Rosé
Errazuriz Estate Cabernet
Sauvignon Rosé 53

Miguel Torres Santa Digna
Cabernet Sauvignon Rosé
Reserve 55

Sparkling

Codorníu Cava Reserva Raventos 132

Jacob's Creek Chardonnay-Pinot Noir Brut Cuvée 135

Jacob's Creek Sparkling Rosé Dry Cuvée 136

Tesco

Elegant, medium-bodied red

Montana East Coast Merlot-Cabernet Sauvignon 71

Light & refreshing white

Montana East Coast Unoaked Chardonnay 20

Tesco Finest Gavi 25

Tesco Finest Steillage Riesling 26

Tesco Finest Tingleup Vineyard Riesling 27

More full-bodied white

Tesco Finest Ken Forrester Chenin Blanc 45

Tesco Finest Oak-Aged White Burgundy 46

Rich full-bodied red

Château Cazal-Viel Saint-Chinian Cuvée des Fées 84

Tesco Argentina Malbec Reserve 119

Tesco Finest Vacqueyras 120

Sparkling

Jacob's Creek Chardonnay-Pinot Noir Brut Cuvée 135

Jacob's Creek Sparkling Rosé Dry Cuvée 136

MAIL ORDER

www.bbr.ie
Elegant, medium-bodied red
Berrys' Good Ordinary Claret 62
More full-bodied white
Monte Del Frà Custoza 42
Sherry
Berrys' Fino Sherry 126

www.enowine.ie
Rich full-bodied red
Domaine Lafond Roc-Épine Côtes
    du Rhône 92
Sparkling
Bortolotti d'Arcàne Prosecco di
    Valdobbiadene Frizzante 130

www.jnwine.com
Rich full-bodied red
Finca Sophenia Altosur Malbec
    98
Norte Chico Merlot 108
T'Air d'Oc Syrah Vin de Pays d'Oc
    117
Rosé
Artazuri Navarra Garnacha
    Rosado 48

www.lecaveau
Light & refreshing white
Alain Brumont Gros Manseng-
    Sauvignon Blanc Vin de Pays
    des Côtes de Gascogne 2

www.louisalbrouze.com
Rich full-bodied red
Château de Bayle Bordeaux 85
Olivier Cuilleras Vin de Pays 109

www.mitchellandson.com
Elegant, medium-bodied red
Mitchell & Son Claret 70
Rich full-bodied red
Paulo Laureano Clássico Vinho
    Regional 110

www.spanishwines.ie
More full-bodied white
Angosto Valencia 34
Rich full-bodied red
Montesierra Tempranillo-
    Cabernet 107

www.wineonline.ie
Light & refreshing white
Alpha Zeta 'P' Pinot Grigio delle
    Venezie 3
La Croix Gratiot Picpoul de Pinet
    Coteaux du Languedoc 17

Rich full-bodied red
Poggio del Sasso Sangiovese di
    Toscana 111

www.winesdirect.ie
Light & refreshing white
Château des Eyssards Bergerac
    Sec 6

Rosé
Domaine Clavel Mescladis Rosé
    Coteaux du Languedoc 52

STOCKISTS BY COUNTY

Clare

Egans Wines, Liscannor
More full-bodied white
Les Perles Viognier Vin de Pays
    d'Oc 37
Rich full-bodied red
Evohé Garnacha Viñas Viejas 95

Jaynes, Ennis
More full-bodied white
Louis Latour Ardèche
    Chardonnay 38
Rich full-bodied red
Domaine de Bisconte Côtes du
    Roussillon 89

Mace, Lisdoonvarna
Sparkling
Moscato d'Asti Ca'Bianca 139

Shannon Knights, Shannon
Elegant, medium-bodied red
Raimat Abadia Crianza 72
Rosso di Valpanera 73

Cork

Bradleys, Cork
Elegant, medium-bodied red
Antinori Santa Cristina Toscana
    61

Cono Sur Pinot Noir 64
Raimat Abadia Crianza 72

Karwig, Carrigaline
More full-bodied white
Les Perles Viognier Vin de Pays
    d'Oc 37
Rich full-bodied red
Evohé Garnacha Viñas Viejas 95

Kitchen Project, Cork
More full-bodied white
Simone Joseph Chardonnay Vin
    de Pays 43

Lynchs, Glanmire
Elegant, medium-bodied red
Rosso di Valpanera 73

O'Donovans outlets
Elegant, medium-bodied red
Chivite Gran Feudo Navarra
    Crianza 63
Cono Sur Pinot Noir 64
Yering Station Little Yering Pinot
    Noir 77
Light & refreshing white
Alpha Zeta 'P' Pinot Grigio delle
    Venezie 3
Devil's Corner Sauvignon Blanc 9

Rich full-bodied red

Domaine des Coccinelles Côtes
du Rhône 90

Finca La Celia La Consulta Malbec
96

Flagstone Fish Hoek Shiraz 99

Hout Bay Shiraz 102

Principe de Viana Navarra
Tempranillo 112

Rocca Ventosa Montepulciano
d'Abruzzo 113

Rosé

Chivite Gran Feudo Navarra
Rosado 50

Errazuriz Estate Cabernet
Sauvignon Rosé 53

Principe de Viana Navarra
Cabernet Sauvignon Rosado
57

Parsons Wines, Carrigaline
Rich full-bodied red

Finca Sophenia Altosur Malbec
98

Donegal

Next Door, Killybegs
Elegant, medium-bodied red
Cono Sur Pinot Noir 64
More full-bodied white
De Wetshof Danie De Wet
Chardonnay Sur Lie 35

Rich full-bodied red

Wakefield Estate Cabernet
Sauvignon 124

Dublin

64 Wine, Glasthule
Light & refreshing white
La Croix Gratiot Picpoul de Pinet
Coteaux du Languedoc 17
More full-bodied white
Les Perles Viognier Vin de Pays
d'Oc 37
Rich full-bodied red
Evohé Garnacha Viñas Viejas 95
Poggio del Sasso Sangiovese di
Toscana 111

Baily Wines, Howth
Elegant, medium-bodied red
Cono Sur Pinot Noir 64

Bennetts, Howth
Elegant, medium-bodied red
Cono Sur Pinot Noir 64
Trapiche Oak Cask Pinot Noir 75
Light & refreshing white
Cusumano Insolia Sicilia 8
Peter Lehmann Barossa Riesling
22
More full-bodied white
Tahbilk Nagambie Lakes
Marsanne 44

Rich full-bodied red
Château Pique-Sègue Bergerac 86
Geoff Merrill Cabernet-Merlot
100
La Ferme du Mont 'Le Ponnant'
Côtes du Rhône Villages 103
Le Petit Jaboulet Syrah Vin de
Pays 104
MAN Vintners Shiraz 105
Wakefield Estate Cabernet
Sauvignon 124
Sparkling
Castillo Perelada Cava Brut
Reserva 131

Berry Bros & Rudd, Harry St,
Elegant, medium-bodied red
Berrys' Good Ordinary Claret 62
More full-bodied white
Monte Del Frà Custoza 42
Sherry
Berrys' Fino Sherry 126

Bin No. 9, Goatstown
Elegant, medium-bodied red
Trapiche Oak Cask Pinot Noir 75
Light & refreshing white
Alpha Zeta 'P' Pinot Grigio delle
Venezie 3
Château Pique-Sègue Montravel
7
Cusumano Insolia Sicilia 8

Rich full-bodied red
Finca La Celia La Consulta Malbec
96
Geoff Merrill Cabernet-Merlot
100
Hout Bay Shiraz 102
Le Petit Jaboulet Syrah Vin de
Pays 104
Poggio del Sasso Sangiovese di
Toscana 111
Principe de Viana Navarra
Tempranillo 112
Rocca Ventosa Montepulciano
d'Abruzzo 113
Rosé
Principe de Viana Navarra
Cabernet Sauvignon Rosado
57
Sparkling
Castillo Perelada Cava Brut
Reserva 131

Boomers, Clondalkin
Light & refreshing white
Château Pique-Sègue Montravel
7

Boozebusters outlets
Rich full-bodied red
Le Petit Jaboulet Syrah Vin de
Pays 104

Bottleshop, Drummartin Rd
Rich full-bodied red
Château de Bayle Bordeaux 85
Olivier Cuilleras Vin de Pays 109

Brackens, Glasnevin
Elegant, medium-bodied red
Rosso di Valpanera 73
Rich full-bodied red
Estampa Reserve Assemblage
    Cabernet Sauvignon-
    Carmenère-Petit Verdot 94

Bradys, Shankill
Rich full-bodied red
Estampa Reserve Assemblage
    Cabernet Sauvignon-
    Carmenère-Petit Verdot 94

**Bradys, Bakers Corner &
Shankill**
Rich full-bodied red
Vega del Castillo Garnacha Cepas
    Viejas 123

Canters, Fairview
Rich full-bodied red
Finca Sophenia Altosur Malbec
    98

Carvills, Camden St
Elegant, medium-bodied red
Trapiche Oak Cask Pinot Noir 75
Rich full-bodied red
Château Pique-Sègue Bergerac 86

Estampa Reserve Assemblage
    Cabernet Sauvignon-
    Carmenère-Petit Verdot 94
Vega del Castillo Garnacha Cepas
    Viejas 123
Sparkling
Castillo Perelada Cava Brut
    Reserva 131

**Cellars Big Wine Warehouse,
Naas Rd**
Elegant, medium-bodied red
Cono Sur Pinot Noir 64
Light & refreshing white
Cusumano Insolia Sicilia 8
Rich full-bodied red
Château Pique-Sègue Bergerac 86
Le Petit Jaboulet Syrah Vin de
    Pays 104
MAN Vintners Shiraz 105
Vega del Castillo Garnacha Cepas
    Viejas 123
Sparkling
Castillo Perelada Cava Brut
    Reserva 131

Cheers outlets
Rosé
Miguel Torres Santa Digna
    Cabernet Sauvignon Rosé
    Reserve 55

Cheers Take Home, Liffey Valley
More full-bodied white
Louis Latour Ardèche
 Chardonnay 38

Coach House, Ballinteer
Elegant, medium-bodied red
Cono Sur Pinot Noir 64
Yering Station Little Yering Pinot
 Noir 77
Light & refreshing white
Château Pique-Sègue Montravel
 7
Devil's Corner Sauvignon Blanc 9
Rich full-bodied red
Domaine des Coccinelles Côtes
 du Rhône 90
Estampa Reserve Assemblage
 Cabernet Sauvignon-
 Carmenère-Petit Verdot 94
Vega del Castillo Garnacha Cepas
 Viejas 123
Wakefield Estate Cabernet
 Sauvignon 124

Comet, Santry
Light & refreshing white
Château Pique-Sègue Montravel
 7
Rich full-bodied red
Château Pique-Sègue Bergerac 86

Geoff Merrill Cabernet-Merlot
 100

Coolers, Applewood
Elegant, medium-bodied red
Cono Sur Pinot Noir 64
Rich full-bodied red
Wakefield Estate Cabernet
 Sauvignon 124

Coolers, Ongar Village
More full-bodied white
Louis Latour Ardèche
 Chardonnay 38

Corks, Terenure
More full-bodied white
Louis Latour Ardèche
 Chardonnay 38
Rich full-bodied red
Château Pique-Sègue Bergerac 86

Corkscrew, Chatham St
Light & refreshing white
Winzer Krems Grüner Veltliner
 Ried Sandgrube 32
More full-bodied white
De Wetshof Danie De Wet
 Chardonnay Sur Lie 35
Rich full-bodied red
La Ferme du Mont 'Le Ponnant'
 Côtes du Rhône Villages 103

Rosé
Artazuri Navarra Garnacha
    Rosado 48
Sparkling
Moscato d'Asti Ca'Bianca 139

Deveneys, Dundrum
More full-bodied white
Tahbilk Nagambie Lakes
    Marsanne 44
Rich full-bodied red
La Ferme du Mont 'Le Ponnant'
    Côtes du Rhône Villages 103
Le Petit Jaboulet Syrah Vin de
    Pays 104
Sparkling
Castillo Perelada Cava Brut
    Reserva 131

Deveneys, Rathmines
Rich full-bodied red
Estampa Reserve Assemblage
    Cabernet Sauvignon-
    Carmenère-Petit Verdot 94
Vega del Castillo Garnacha Cepas
    Viejas 123
Sparkling
Castillo Perelada Cava Brut
    Reserva 131

Donnybrook Fair,
Donnybrook
Elegant, medium-bodied red
Trapiche Oak Cask Pinot Noir 75

Light & refreshing white
Alpha Zeta 'P' Pinot Grigio delle
    Venezie 3
Château Pique-Sègue Montravel
    7
Cusumano Insolia Sicilia 8
La Croix Gratiot Picpoul de Pinet
    Coteaux du Languedoc 17
Peter Lehmann Barossa Riesling
    22
More full-bodied white
Tahbilk Nagambie Lakes
    Marsanne 44
Rich full-bodied red
Botalcura Syrah-Malbec Reserva
    El Delirio 82
Château Pique-Sègue Bergerac 86
Finca La Celia La Consulta Malbec
    96
Geoff Merrill Cabernet-Merlot
    100
Hout Bay Shiraz 102
Le Petit Jaboulet Syrah Vin de
    Pays 104
Poggio del Sasso Sangiovese di
    Toscana 111
Principe de Viana Navarra
    Tempranillo 112
Rocca Ventosa Montepulciano
    d'Abruzzo 113

Rosé
Principe de Viana Navarra
Cabernet Sauvignon Rosado
57
Sparkling
Castillo Perelada Cava Brut
Reserva 131

Donohoes, College St
Elegant, medium-bodied red
Mitchell & Son Claret 70

Drink Store, Manor St
Light & refreshing white
Alpha Zeta 'P' Pinot Grigio delle
Venezie 3
More full-bodied white
Simone Joseph Chardonnay Vin
de Pays 43
Tahbilk Nagambie Lakes
Marsanne 44
Rich full-bodied red
Botalcura Syrah-Malbec Reserva
El Delirio 82
Château Pique-Sègue Bergerac 86
Finca Sophenia Altosur Malbec
98
Poggio del Sasso Sangiovese di
Toscana 111
Rosé
Artazuri Navarra Garnacha
Rosado 48

Sparkling
Castillo Perelada Cava Brut
Reserva 131

Enowine, IFSC & Monkstown
Light & refreshing white
Alpha Zeta 'P' Pinot Grigio delle
Venezie 3
La Croix Gratiot Picpoul de Pinet
Coteaux du Languedoc 17
Rich full-bodied red
Domaine Lafond Roc-Épine Côtes
du Rhône 92
Poggio del Sasso Sangiovese di
Toscana 111
Sparkling
Bortolotti d'Arcàne Prosecco di
Valdobbiadene Frizzante 130

Eurospar, Rathcoole
Elegant, medium-bodied red
Trapiche Oak Cask Pinot Noir 75
Light & refreshing white
Château Pique-Sègue Montravel
7
Peter Lehmann Barossa Riesling
22
More full-bodied white
Tahbilk Nagambie Lakes
Marsanne 44
Rich full-bodied red
Château Pique-Sègue Bergerac 86

Sparkling
Castillo Perelada Cava Brut
Reserva 131

Eurospar, Smithfield
Elegant, medium-bodied red
Raimat Abadia Crianza 72

Fallon & Byrne, Exchequer St
Elegant, medium-bodied red
Corinto Merlot 65
Light & refreshing white
Alpha Zeta 'P' Pinot Grigio delle
Venezie 3
Rich full-bodied red
Evohé Garnacha Viñas Viejas 95
Poggio del Sasso Sangiovese di
Toscana 111

Flanagans, Harold's Cross
Rich full-bodied red
Goats Do Roam 101

Fresh, Grand Canal
Rich full-bodied red
La Ferme du Mont 'Le Ponnant'
Côtes du Rhône Villages 103

Fresh, Northern Cross
Rich full-bodied red
La Ferme du Mont 'Le Ponnant'
Côtes du Rhône Villages 103

Fresh, Smithfield
Rich full-bodied red
La Ferme du Mont 'Le Ponnant'
Côtes du Rhône Villages 103

Gibneys, Malahide
Light & refreshing white
Château Pique-Sègue Montravel
7
Winzer Krems Grüner Veltliner
Ried Sandgrube 32
More full-bodied white
Les Perles Viognier Vin de Pays
d'Oc 37
Tahbilk Nagambie Lakes
Marsanne 44
Rich full-bodied red
Château Pique-Sègue Bergerac 86
Estampa Reserve Assemblage
Cabernet Sauvignon-
Carmenère-Petit Verdot 94
Evohé Garnacha Viñas Viejas 95
Principe de Viana Navarra
Tempranillo 112
Rosé
Principe de Viana Navarra
Cabernet Sauvignon Rosado
57
Sparkling
Castillo Perelada Cava Brut
Reserva 131

Goggins, Monkstown
Rich full-bodied red
Finca Sophenia Altosur Malbec
  98
Rosé
Artazuri Navarra Garnacha
  Rosado 48

Goose, Drumcondra
Elegant, medium-bodied red
Trapiche Oak Cask Pinot Noir 75
Yering Station Little Yering Pinot
  Noir 77
Light & refreshing white
Château Pique-Sègue Montravel
  7
Devil's Corner Sauvignon Blanc 9
More full-bodied white
Tahbilk Nagambie Lakes
  Marsanne 44
Rich full-bodied red
Château Pique-Sègue Bergerac 86
Domaine des Coccinelles Côtes
  du Rhône 90
Estampa Reserve Assemblage
  Cabernet Sauvignon-
  Carmenère-Petit Verdot 94
Geoff Merrill Cabernet-Merlot
  100
Sparkling
Castillo Perelada Cava Brut
  Reserva 131

Higgins, Clonskeagh
Elegant, medium-bodied red
Trapiche Oak Cask Pinot Noir 75
More full-bodied white
Tahbilk Nagambie Lakes
  Marsanne 44
Rich full-bodied red
Château Pique-Sègue Bergerac 86
Geoff Merrill Cabernet-Merlot
  100
Sparkling
Castillo Perelada Cava Brut
  Reserva 131

Hole in the Wall, Blackhorse Ave
Light & refreshing white
Alpha Zeta 'P' Pinot Grigio delle
  Venezie 3
Winzer Krems Grüner Veltliner
  Ried Sandgrube 32
Rich full-bodied red
Estampa Reserve Assemblage
  Cabernet Sauvignon-
  Carmenère-Petit Verdot 94
Poggio del Sasso Sangiovese di
  Toscana 111

Jus de Vine, Portmarnock
Elegant, medium-bodied red
Cono Sur Pinot Noir 64
Trapiche Oak Cask Pinot Noir 75

Listons, Camden St
Rich full-bodied red
Domaine de Bisconte Côtes du
    Roussillon 89

Liz Delaneys, Coolock
Rich full-bodied red
MAN Vintners Shiraz 105

Londis, Malahide
Elegant, medium-bodied red
Rosso di Valpanera 73
Trapiche Oak Cask Pinot Noir 75
Rich full-bodied red
Geoff Merrill Cabernet-Merlot
    100

**Louis Albrouze, Upper Leeson
St**
Rich full-bodied red
Château de Bayle Bordeaux 85
Olivier Cuilleras Vin de Pays 109

Malt House, James' St
Light & refreshing white
Alpha Zeta 'P' Pinot Grigio delle
    Venezie 3
La Croix Gratiot Picpoul de Pinet
    Coteaux du Languedoc 17

**Marthas Vineyard,
Rathfarnham**
Elegant, medium-bodied red
Trapiche Oak Cask Pinot Noir 75

Rich full-bodied red
Goats Do Roam 101
MAN Vintners Shiraz 105

Martins, Fairview
Elegant, medium-bodied red
Rosso di Valpanera 73
Rich full-bodied red
La Ferme du Mont 'Le Ponnant'
    Côtes du Rhône Villages 103

Martins, Marino
Rosé
Artazuri Navarra Garnacha
    Rosado 48

**Masseys Costcutter,
Rathfarnham**
Elegant, medium-bodied red
Rosso di Valpanera 73

McCabes, Blackrock
Elegant, medium-bodied red
Yering Station Little Yering Pinot
    Noir 77
Light & refreshing white
Cusumano Insolia Sicilia 8
Devil's Corner Sauvignon Blanc 9
More full-bodied white
Simone Joseph Chardonnay Vin
    de Pays 43
Rich full-bodied red
Domaine des Coccinelles Côtes
    du Rhône 90

Finca La Celia La Consulta Malbec
96
Hout Bay Shiraz 102
Le Petit Jaboulet Syrah Vin de
Pays 104
MAN Vintners Shiraz 105
Principe de Viana Navarra
Tempranillo 112
Rocca Ventosa Montepulciano
d'Abruzzo 113
Rosé
Miguel Torres Santa Digna
Cabernet Sauvignon Rosé
Reserve 55
Principe de Viana Navarra
Cabernet Sauvignon Rosado
57
Torres de Casta Rosada 58

McCabes, Foxrock
Light & refreshing white
Cusumano Insolia Sicilia 8
Rich full-bodied red
Finca La Celia La Consulta Malbec
96
Hout Bay Shiraz 102
Le Petit Jaboulet Syrah Vin de
Pays 104
MAN Vintners Shiraz 105
Principe de Viana Navarra
Tempranillo 112
Rocca Ventosa Montepulciano
d'Abruzzo 113

Rosé
Principe de Viana Navarra
Cabernet Sauvignon Rosado
57

**McHughs, Artane &
Kilbarrack**
Elegant, medium-bodied red
Yering Station Little Yering Pinot
Noir 77
Light & refreshing white
Cusumano Insolia Sicilia 8
Devil's Corner Sauvignon Blanc 9
Rich full-bodied red
Domaine des Coccinelles Côtes
du Rhône 90
Flagstone Fish Hoek Shiraz 99
Le Petit Jaboulet Syrah Vin de
Pays 104
MAN Vintners Shiraz 105
Rosé
Errazuriz Estate Cabernet
Sauvignon Rosé 53

**Michaels Wines, Mount
Merrion**
More full-bodied white
Les Perles Viognier Vin de Pays
d'Oc 37
Rich full-bodied red
Evohé Garnacha Viñas Viejas 95

Rosé

Artazuri Navarra Garnacha
Rosado 48

**Mitchell & Son, CHQ Building
IFSC, Glasthule &
Rathfarnham**

Elegant, medium-bodied red

Mitchell & Son Claret 70

More full-bodied white

Les Perles Viognier Vin de Pays
d'Oc 37

Rich full-bodied red

Evohé Garnacha Viñas Viejas 95
Flagstone Fish Hoek Shiraz 99
Paulo Laureano Clássico Vinho
Regional 110

Rosé

Errazuriz Estate Cabernet
Sauvignon Rosé 53
Miguel Torres Santa Digna
Cabernet Sauvignon Rosé
Reserve 55

Molloys outlets

Elegant, medium-bodied red

Antinori Santa Cristina Toscana
61
Chivite Gran Feudo Navarra
Crianza 63
Cono Sur Pinot Noir 64
Montana East Coast Merlot-
Cabernet Sauvignon 71

Light & refreshing white

Château Pique-Sègue Montravel
7
Peter Lehmann Barossa Riesling
22

Rich full-bodied red

Château Pique-Sègue Bergerac 86
Flagstone Fish Hoek Shiraz 99
Geoff Merrill Cabernet-Merlot
100

Rosé

Chivite Gran Feudo Navarra
Rosado 50
Errazuriz Estate Cabernet
Sauvignon Rosé 53
Torres de Casta Rosada 58

Sparkling

Castillo Perelada Cava Brut
Reserva 131
Jacob's Creek Chardonnay-Pinot
Noir Brut Cuvée 135
Jacob's Creek Sparkling Rosé Dry
Cuvée 136

Mortons, Firhouse

Elegant, medium-bodied red

Rosso di Valpanera 73

Mortons, Ranelagh

More full-bodied white

Tahbilk Nagambie Lakes
Marsanne 44

Rich full-bodied red
Botalcura Syrah-Malbec Reserva
  El Delirio 82
Château de Bayle Bordeaux 85
Flagstone Fish Hoek Shiraz 99
Olivier Cuilleras Vin de Pays 109
Rosé
Errazuriz Estate Cabernet
  Sauvignon Rosé 53
Sparkling
Castillo Perelada Cava Brut
  Reserva 131

Nolans, Clontarf
More full-bodied white
Louis Latour Ardèche
  Chardonnay 38
Rich full-bodied red
La Ferme du Mont 'Le Ponnant'
  Côtes du Rhône Villages 103

**On the Grapevine,
Booterstown**
Elegant, medium-bodied red
Corinto Merlot 65
Trapiche Oak Cask Pinot Noir 75
Rich full-bodied red
Domaine de Biscontes Côtes du
  Roussillon 89
Sparkling
Castillo Perelada Cava Brut
  Reserva 131

On the Grapevine, Dalkey
Elegant, medium-bodied red
Trapiche Oak Cask Pinot Noir 75
Sparkling
Castillo Perelada Cava Brut
  Reserva 131

O'Neills, SCR
Elegant, medium-bodied red
Trapiche Oak Cask Pinot Noir 75
Light & refreshing white
Château Pique-Sègue Montravel
  7
More full-bodied white
Tahbilk Nagambie Lakes
  Marsanne 44
Rich full-bodied red
Geoff Merrill Cabernet-Merlot
  100

Orchard, Applewood
Elegant, medium-bodied red
Trapiche Oak Cask Pinot Noir 75
Light & refreshing white
Château Pique-Sègue Montravel
  7

Quinns, Drumcondra
More full-bodied white
Louis Latour Ardèche
  Chardonnay 38

Red Island Wines, Skerries
Elegant, medium-bodied red
Corinto Merlot 65
Trapiche Oak Cask Pinot Noir 75
Light & refreshing white
Alpha Zeta 'P' Pinot Grigio delle
   Venezie 3
Peter Lehmann Barossa Riesling
   22
Rich full-bodied red
Geoff Merrill Cabernet-Merlot
   100
Poggio del Sasso Sangiovese di
   Toscana 111
Sparkling
Castillo Perelada Cava Brut
   Reserva 131

Redmonds, Ranelagh
Elegant, medium-bodied red
Antinori Santa Cristina Toscana
   61
Cono Sur Pinot Noir 64
Trapiche Oak Cask Pinot Noir 75
Yering Station Little Yering Pinot
   Noir 77
Light & refreshing white
Château Pique-Sègue Montravel
   7
Devil's Corner Sauvignon Blanc 9
Peter Lehmann Barossa Riesling
   22

Winzer Krems Grüner Veltliner
   Ried Sandgrube 32
More full-bodied white
Simone Joseph Chardonnay Vin
   de Pays 43
Tahbilk Nagambie Lakes
   Marsanne 44
Rich full-bodied red
Château Pique-Sègue Bergerac 86
Domaine des Coccinelles Côtes
   du Rhône 90
Evohé Garnacha Viñas Viejas 95
Finca Sophenia Altosur Malbec
   98
Flagstone Fish Hoek Shiraz 99
La Ferme du Mont 'Le Ponnant'
   Côtes du Rhône Villages 103
Rosé
Errazuriz Estate Cabernet
   Sauvignon Rosé 53
Sparkling
Castillo Perelada Cava Brut
   Reserva 131

Savages, Swords
More full-bodied white
Louis Latour Ardèche
   Chardonnay 38

Searsons, Monkstown
Elegant, medium-bodied red
Corinto Merlot 65

Rich full-bodied red
Botalcura Syrah-Malbec Reserva
   El Delirio 82
Domaine de Bisconte Côtes du
   Roussillon 89

Sheils, Dorset St
Elegant, medium-bodied red
Raimat Abadia Crianza 72
Rosso di Valpanera 73
Rich full-bodied red
La Ferme du Mont 'Le Ponnant'
   Côtes du Rhône Villages 103

Silver Granite, Palmerstown
More full-bodied white
Louis Latour Ardèche
   Chardonnay 38

SPAR, Ballycullen
Elegant, medium-bodied red
Trapiche Oak Cask Pinot Noir 75
Rich full-bodied red
Geoff Merrill Cabernet-Merlot
   100

SPAR, Carpenterstown
Light & refreshing white
Winzer Krems Grüner Veltliner
   Ried Sandgrube 32

Strand, Fairview
Rich full-bodied red
La Ferme du Mont 'Le Ponnant'
   Côtes du Rhône Villages 103

**SuperValu/Centra,
Churchtown**
Elegant, medium-bodied red
Rosso di Valpanera 73

SuperValu/Centra, Raheny
Sparkling
Castillo Perelada Cava Brut
   Reserva 131

Sweeneys, Glasnevin
More full-bodied white
De Wetshof Danie De Wet
   Chardonnay Sur Lie 35
Les Perles Viognier Vin de Pays
   d'Oc 37
Rich full-bodied red
Evohé Garnacha Viñas Viejas 95
Finca La Celia La Consulta Malbec
   96
Finca Sophenia Altosur Malbec
   98
Hout Bay Shiraz 102
La Ferme du Mont 'Le Ponnant'
   Côtes du Rhône Villages 103
Principe de Viana Navarra
   Tempranillo 112
Rocca Ventosa Montepulciano
   d'Abruzzo 113
Rosé
Principe de Viana Navarra
   Cabernet Sauvignon Rosado
   57

Thomas Deli, Foxrock
Rich full-bodied red
Finca La Celia La Consulta Malbec
96
Hout Bay Shiraz 102
La Ferme du Mont 'Le Ponnant'
Côtes du Rhône Villages 103
Principe de Viana Navarra
Tempranillo 112
Rocca Ventosa Montepulciano
d'Abruzzo 113
Rosé
Principe de Viana Navarra
Cabernet Sauvignon Rosado
57

Uncorked, Rathfarnham
Elegant, medium-bodied red
Corinto Merlot 65

Unwined, Swords
Light & refreshing white
Peter Lehmann Barossa Riesling
22
More full-bodied white
Les Perles Viognier Vin de Pays
d'Oc 37
Tahbilk Nagambie Lakes
Marsanne 44
Rich full-bodied red
Château Pique-Sègue Bergerac 86
Evohé Garnacha Viñas Viejas 95

Geoff Merrill Cabernet-Merlot
100
Sparkling
Castillo Perelada Cava Brut
Reserva 131

Vintry, Rathgar
Elegant, medium-bodied red
Raimat Abadia Crianza 72
Trapiche Oak Cask Pinot Noir 75
Light & refreshing white
Château Pique-Sègue Montravel
7
Peter Lehmann Barossa Riesling
22
More full-bodied white
Tahbilk Nagambie Lakes
Marsanne 44
Rich full-bodied red
Château Pique-Sègue Bergerac 86
Flagstone Fish Hoek Shiraz 99
Rosé
Errazuriz Estate Cabernet
Sauvignon Rosé 53

Walsh Wines, Dun Laoghaire
Rich full-bodied red
Vega del Castillo Garnacha Cepas
Viejas 123

Whelans, Wexford St
Rich full-bodied red
Principe de Viana Navarra
Tempranillo 112

Wilde & Green, Milltown
Rich full-bodied red
La Ferme du Mont 'Le Ponnant'
  Côtes du Rhône Villages 103

Galway

Cases Wine Warehouse, Galway
Light & refreshing white
Winzer Krems Grüner Veltliner
  Ried Sandgrube 32
More full-bodied white
Simone Joseph Chardonnay Vin
  de Pays 43

Guys Wine Shop, Galway
Rosé
Artazuri Navarra Garnacha
  Rosado 48

Harvest outlets
Elegant, medium-bodied red
Cono Sur Pinot Noir 64
Light & refreshing white
Cusumano Insolia Sicilia 8
More full-bodied white
Louis Latour Ardèche
  Chardonnay 38
Rich full-bodied red
Le Petit Jaboulet Syrah Vin de
  Pays 104
MAN Vintners Shiraz 105
Santa Julia Malbec 116

Wakefield Estate Cabernet
  Sauvignon 124

Joyces, Athenry
Elegant, medium-bodied red
Raimat Abadia Crianza 72

Joyces, Galway & Headford
Elegant, medium-bodied red
Antinori Santa Cristina Toscana
  61
Cono Sur Pinot Noir 64
Rich full-bodied red
Wakefield Estate Cabernet
  Sauvignon 124

Mad About Wine, Moycullen
Rich full-bodied red
Finca Sophenia Altosur Malbec
  98

Mortons, Salthill
Rosé
Artazuri Navarra Garnacha
  Rosado 48
Rich full-bodied red
Botalcura Syrah-Malbec Reserva
  El Delirio 82
Château de Bayle Bordeaux 85
Olivier Cuilleras Vin de Pays 109

Salthill Liquor Store, Salthill
Elegant, medium-bodied red
Yering Station Little Yering Pinot
  Noir 77

Light & refreshing white
Devil's Corner Sauvignon Blanc 9
Rich full-bodied red
Domaine des Coccinelles Côtes
du Rhône 90

Vineyard, Galway
Light & refreshing white
Château Pique-Sègue Montravel
7
Peter Lehmann Barossa Riesling
22
More full-bodied white
Tahbilk Nagambie Lakes
Marsanne 44
Rich full-bodied red
Château Pique-Sègue Bergerac 86
Sparkling
Castillo Perelada Cava Brut
Reserva 131

Kerry

Centra, Killorgan
Rich full-bodied red
Goats Do Roam 101

Kingdom Stores, Tralee
More full-bodied white
Les Perles Viognier Vin de Pays
d'Oc 37
Rich full-bodied red
Evohé Garnacha Viñas Viejas 95

Finca La Celia La Consulta Malbec
96
Hout Bay Shiraz 102
Principe de Viana Navarra
Tempranillo 112
Rocca Ventosa Montepulciano
d'Abruzzo 113
Rosé
Principe de Viana Navarra
Cabernet Sauvignon Rosado
57

Vanilla Grape, Kenmare
More full-bodied white
Simone Joseph Chardonnay Vin
de Pays 43

Kildare

Applegreen, Newbridge
Light & refreshing white
Peter Lehmann Barossa Riesling
22

Mill Wine Cellar, Maynooth
Elegant, medium-bodied red
Trapiche Oak Cask Pinot Noir 75
Yering Station Little Yering Pinot
Noir 77
Light & refreshing white
Château Pique-Sègue Montravel
7
Devil's Corner Sauvignon Blanc 9

Peter Lehmann Barossa Riesling
22
More full-bodied white
Tahbilk Nagambie Lakes
Marsanne 44
Rich full-bodied red
Château Pique-Sègue Bergerac 86
Domaine des Coccinelles Côtes
du Rhône 90
Estampa Reserve Assemblage
Cabernet Sauvignon-
Carmenère-Petit Verdot 94
Geoff Merrill Cabernet-Merlot
100
Sparkling
Castillo Perelada Cava Brut
Reserva 131

Next Door, Clane
Rich full-bodied red
Le Petit Jaboulet Syrah Vin de
Pays 104

O'Rourkes, Newbridge
More full-bodied white
De Wetshof Danie De Wet
Chardonnay Sur Lie 35
Sparkling
Moscato d'Asti Ca'Bianca 139

Swans on the Green, Naas
Rich full-bodied red
Botalcura Syrah-Malbec Reserva
El Delirio 82

La Ferme du Mont 'Le Ponnant'
Côtes du Rhône Villages 103

Kilkenny

Le Caveau, Kilkenny
Light & refreshing white
Alain Brumont Gros Manseng-
Sauvignon Blanc Vin de Pays
des Côtes de Gascogne 2
Alpha Zeta 'P' Pinot Grigio delle
Venezie 3
Rich full-bodied red
Poggio del Sasso Sangiovese di
Toscana 111

Next Door, Thomastown
Rich full-bodied red
Evohé Garnacha Viñas Viejas 95

Wine Centre, Kilkenny
Elegant, medium-bodied red
Raimat Abadia Crianza 72

Laois

Egans, Portlaoise
Light & refreshing white
Cusumano Insolia Sicilia 8
Rich full-bodied red
Le Petit Jaboulet Syrah Vin de
Pays 104
MAN Vintners Shiraz 105

Portlaoise Wine Vault, Portlaoise
Elegant, medium-bodied red
Raimat Abadia Crianza 72
Rich full-bodied red
Santa Julia Malbec 116

Limerick

Fine Wines, Limerick
Rich full-bodied red
Goats Do Roam 101

Louth

Callans, Dundalk
Elegant, medium-bodied red
Rosso di Valpanera 73
Light & refreshing white
Cusumano Insolia Sicilia 8
Rich full-bodied red
Domaine Lafond Roc-Épine Côtes
    du Rhône 92
Le Petit Jaboulet Syrah Vin de
    Pays 104
MAN Vintners Shiraz 105
Sparkling
Bortolotti d'Arcàne Prosecco di
    Valdobbiadene Frizzante 130

Egans, Drogheda
Rich full-bodied red
Domaine Lafond Roc-Épine Côtes
    du Rhône 92

Sparkling
Bortolotti d'Arcàne Prosecco di
    Valdobbiadene Frizzante 130

Shermans Off-Licence, Dunleer
Rich full-bodied red
MAN Vintners Shiraz 105

Mayo

Fahys, Ballina
Rosé
Artazuri Navarra Garnacha
    Rosado 48

Meath

Bunch of Grapes, Clonee
Elegant, medium-bodied red
Cono Sur Pinot Noir 64
Trapiche Oak Cask Pinot Noir 75
Light & refreshing white
Château Pique-Sègue Montravel
    7
Peter Lehmann Barossa Riesling
    22
More full-bodied white
De Wetshof Danie De Wet
    Chardonnay Sur Lie 35
Rich full-bodied red
Château Pique-Sègue Bergerac 86

Estampa Reserve Assemblage
Cabernet Sauvignon-
Carmenère-Petit Verdot 94
Wakefield Estate Cabernet
Sauvignon 124

Carrolls, Kells
Elegant, medium-bodied red
Cono Sur Pinot Noir 64

Cashel Wine Cellar, Navan
Elegant, medium-bodied red
Corinto Merlot 65
Raimat Abadia Crianza 72

Centra, Navan
Rich full-bodied red
Goats Do Roam 101

Coolers, Ongar Village
Light & refreshing white
Winzer Krems Grüner Veltliner
Ried Sandgrube 32
Sparkling
Castillo Perelada Cava Brut
Reserva 131

Dew Drop, Athboy
Sparkling
Moscato d'Asti Ca'Bianca 139

Gardenworks, Dunboyne
Elegant, medium-bodied red
Rosso di Valpanera 73

Next Door, Enfield
Elegant, medium-bodied red
Cono Sur Pinot Noir 64
Light & refreshing white
Château Pique-Sègue Montravel
7
Peter Lehmann Barossa Riesling
22
More full-bodied white
De Wetshof Danie De Wet
Chardonnay Sur Lie 35
Rich full-bodied red
Geoff Merrill Cabernet-Merlot
100
Sparkling
Castillo Perelada Cava Brut
Reserva 131
Moscato d'Asti Ca'Bianca 139

O'Dwyers, Navan
Rich full-bodied red
Domaine Lafond Roc-Épine Côtes
du Rhône 92
Sparkling
Bortolotti d'Arcàne Prosecco di
Valdobbiadene Frizzante 130

Round O, Navan
Elegant, medium-bodied red
Rosso di Valpanera 73

Offaly

Lynchs Bottleshop, Tullamore
Light & refreshing white
Cusumano Insolia Sicilia 8
Rich full-bodied red
Le Petit Jaboulet Syrah Vin de
Pays 104
MAN Vintners Shiraz 105

Roscommon

Clarkes, Boyle
Rich full-bodied red
Wakefield Estate Cabernet
Sauvignon 124

Dalys, Boyle
Elegant, medium-bodied red
Trapiche Oak Cask Pinot Noir 75
Light & refreshing white
Château Pique-Sègue Montravel
7
Peter Lehmann Barossa Riesling
22
More full-bodied white
Tahbilk Nagambie Lakes
Marsanne 44
Rich full-bodied red
Château Pique-Sègue Bergerac 86
Geoff Merrill Cabernet-Merlot
100

Sparkling
Castillo Perelada Cava Brut
Reserva 131

Sligo

Currids, Sligo
Elegant, medium-bodied red
Yering Station Little Yering Pinot
Noir 77
Light & refreshing white
Devil's Corner Sauvignon Blanc 9
Rich full-bodied red
Domaine des Coccinelles Côtes
du Rhône 90

Patrick Stewart Wines, Sligo
Elegant, medium-bodied red
Corinto Merlot 65

Tipperary

Coopers, Tipperary
Elegant, medium-bodied red
Cono Sur Pinot Noir 64

Eldons, Clonmel
Elegant, medium-bodied red
Cono Sur Pinot Noir 64
Raimat Abadia Crianza 72
Light & refreshing white
Cusumano Insolia Sicilia 8

Rich full-bodied red
La Ferme du Mont 'Le Ponnant'
  Côtes du Rhône Villages 103
Le Petit Jaboulet Syrah Vin de
  Pays 104
MAN Vintners Shiraz 105

Kellers Take Home, Roscrea
Elegant, medium-bodied red
Yering Station Little Yering Pinot
  Noir 77
Light & refreshing white
Devil's Corner Sauvignon Blanc 9
Rich full-bodied red
Domaine des Coccinelles Côtes
  du Rhône 90

Lonergans, Clonmel
Elegant, medium-bodied red
Trapiche Oak Cask Pinot Noir 75
Yering Station Little Yering Pinot
  Noir 77
Light & refreshing white
Château Pique-Sègue Montravel
  7
Cusumano Insolia Sicilia 8
Devil's Corner Sauvignon Blanc 9
Peter Lehmann Barossa Riesling
  22
Rich full-bodied red
Château Pique-Sègue Bergerac 86
Domaine des Coccinelles Côtes
  du Rhône 90

Le Petit Jaboulet Syrah Vin de
  Pays 104
MAN Vintners Shiraz 105
Sparkling
Castillo Perelada Cava Brut
  Reserva 131

Waterford

Ardkeen Stores, Waterford
Elegant, medium-bodied red
Antinori Santa Cristina Toscana
  61
Cono Sur Pinot Noir 64
Light & refreshing white
Château Pique-Sègue Montravel
  7
Cusumano Insolia Sicilia 8
Peter Lehmann Barossa Riesling
  22
More full-bodied white
Les Perles Viognier Vin de Pays
  d'Oc 37
Rich full-bodied red
Château Pique-Sègue Bergerac 86
Domaine de Bisconte Côtes du
  Roussillon 89
Evohé Garnacha Viñas Viejas 95
Le Petit Jaboulet Syrah Vin de
  Pays 104
MAN Vintners Shiraz 105
Wakefield Estate Cabernet
  Sauvignon 124

Sparkling
Castillo Perelada Cava Brut
    Reserva 131

Florries Fine Wines, Tramore
Light & refreshing white
La Croix Gratiot Picpoul de Pinet
    Coteaux du Languedoc 17

**Flynns Bar & Off Licence,
Waterford**
More full-bodied white
Louis Latour Ardèche
    Chardonnay 38

Garveys, Waterford
Rich full-bodied red
Domaine de Bisconte Côtes du
    Roussillon 89

Oskars Wine Shop, Waterford
Elegant, medium-bodied red
Corinto Merlot 65

Wine Vaults, Lismore
Sparkling
Moscato d'Asti Ca'Bianca 139

Worldwine Wines, Waterford
Elegant, medium-bodied red
Raimat Abadia Crianza 72
Yering Station Little Yering Pinot
    Noir 77

Light & refreshing white
Cusumano Insolia Sicilia 8

Devil's Corner Sauvignon Blanc 9
Rich full-bodied red
Château de Bayle Bordeaux 85
Domaine des Coccinelles Côtes
    du Rhône 90
Finca Sophenia Altosur Malbec
    98
Le Petit Jaboulet Syrah Vin de
    Pays 104
MAN Vintners Shiraz 105
Olivier Cuilleras Vin de Pays 109

Wexford

Greenacres, Wexford
Light & refreshing white
Cusumano Insolia Sicilia 8
Rich full-bodied red
Le Petit Jaboulet Syrah Vin de
    Pays 104
MAN Vintners Shiraz 105

Myles Doyles, Gorey
Elegant, medium-bodied red
Mitchell & Son Claret 70

Reids, Enniscorthy
Elegant, medium-bodied red
Rosso di Valpanera 73

Wicklow

Capranis, Ashford
Elegant, medium-bodied red
Yering Station Little Yering Pinot
    Noir 77
Light & refreshing white
Devil's Corner Sauvignon Blanc 9
Rich full-bodied red
Domaine des Coccinelles Côtes
    du Rhône 90

Emilias Fine Food & Wine, Enniskerry
Rich full-bodied red
Botalcura Syrah-Malbec Reserva
    El Delirio 82

Hollands, Bray
Elegant, medium-bodied red
Rosso di Valpanera 73
Trapiche Oak Cask Pinot Noir 75
Yering Station Little Yering Pinot
    Noir 77
Light & refreshing white
Cusumano Insolia Sicilia 8
Devil's Corner Sauvignon Blanc 9
Peter Lehmann Barossa Riesling
    22
More full-bodied white
Tahbilk Nagambie Lakes
    Marsanne 44

Rich full-bodied red
Château Pique-Sègue Bergerac 86
Domaine des Coccinelles Côtes
    du Rhône 90
Estampa Reserve Assemblage
    Cabernet Sauvignon-
    Carmenère-Petit Verdot 94
Finca Sophenia Altosur Malbec
    98
Geoff Merrill Cabernet-Merlot
    100
Le Petit Jaboulet Syrah Vin de
    Pays 104
MAN Vintners Shiraz 105

Kings, Delgany
Rich full-bodied red
Domaine Lafond Roc-Épine Côtes
    du Rhône 92
Sparkling
Bortolotti d'Arcàne Prosecco di
    Valdobbiadene Frizzante 130

Next Door, Blessington
Rich full-bodied red
Goats Do Roam 101

Quinns, Baltinglass
More full-bodied white
Louis Latour Ardèche
    Chardonnay 38

Roundwood Food and Wine, Roundwood
Rich full-bodied red
T'Air d'Oc Syrah Vin de Pays d'Oc 117

Wicklow Arms, Delgany
Light & refreshing white
Château Pique-Sègue Montravel 7
Winzer Krems Grüner Veltliner Ried Sandgrube 32
More full-bodied white
Tahbilk Nagambie Lakes Marsanne 44

Rich full-bodied red
La Ferme du Mont 'Le Ponnant' Côtes du Rhône Villages 103
Sparkling
Castillo Perelada Cava Brut Reserva 131

Wicklow Wine Co., Wicklow
Rich full-bodied red
Evohé Garnacha Viñas Viejas 95
Flagstone Fish Hoek Shiraz 99
Rosé
Errazuriz Estate Cabernet Sauvignon Rosé 53

INDEX
OF
WINES

WINES
BY
GRAPE

Corvina, Rondinella, Molinara

Marks & Spencer Ripasso Valpolicella Classico 106

Corvina, Rondinella, Sangiovese

Guerrieri-Rizzardi Rosa Rosae Rosato 54

Fiano

Inycon Estate Fiano Sicilia 14

Gamay, Pinot Noir

Marks & Spencer Mâcon Rouge 69

Garganega

Monte Del Frà Custoza 42

Garnacha

Artazuri Navarra Garnacha Rosado 48

Chivite Gran Feudo Navarra Rosado 50

Evohé Garnacha Viñas Viejas 95

Vega del Castillo Garnacha Cepas Viejas 123

Garnacha, Cariñena

Torres de Casta Rosada 58

Grenache, Syrah

Domaine Grès Saint Vincent Côtes du Rhône Villages Sinargues 91

Domaine Lafond Roc-Épine Côtes du Rhône 92

La Ferme du Mont 'Le Ponnant' Côtes du Rhône Villages 103

Olivier Cuilleras Vin de Pays 109

Grenache, Syrah, Mourvèdre

Tesco Finest Vacqueyras 120

Grenache, Syrah, Mourvèdre, Cinsault

Domaine des Coccinelles Côtes du Rhône 90

Gros Manseng, Sauvignon Blanc

Alain Brumont Gros Manseng-Sauvignon Blanc Vin de Pays des Côtes de Gascogne 2

Grüner Veltliner

Dolle Grüner Veltliner Strassertal 36

Winzer Krems Grüner Veltliner Ried Sandgrube 32

Insolia

Cusumano Insolia Sicilia 8

Mainly Syrah

Château Cazal-Viel Saint-Chinian Cuvée des Fées 84

Malbec

Bodega Norton Barrel Select Malbec 81

Finca La Celia La Consulta Malbec 96

Finca Sophenia Altosur Malbec 98

Shiraz

Flagstone Fish Hoek Shiraz 99
Hout Bay Shiraz 102
MAN Vintners Shiraz 105

Shiraz, Pinotage, Cinsault, Mourvèdre, Grenache, Carignan

Goats Do Roam 101

Syrah

Carmen Syrah 83
Le Petit Jaboulet Syrah Vin de Pays 104
T'Air d'Oc Syrah Vin de Pays d'Oc 117

Syrah, Cinsault

Domaine Clavel Mescladis Rosé Coteaux du Languedoc 52

Syrah, Grenache, Carignan

Domaine de Bisconte Côtes du Roussillon 89

Syrah, Malbec

Botalcura Syrah-Malbec Reserva El Delirio 82

Syrah, Mourvèdre, Viognier

The Wolftrap Syrah-Mourvèdre-Viognier 122

Tempranillo

Finca Labarca Rioja Crianza 97
Principe de Viana Navarra Tempranillo 112

Tempranillo, Cabernet Sauvignon

Bestué de Otto Bestué Somontano Finca Rableros 80

Tempranillo, Cabernet Sauvignon, Moristel

Montesierra Tempranillo-Cabernet 107

Tempranillo, Garnacha, Cabernet Sauvignon

Chivite Gran Feudo Navarra Crianza 63

Tinta Roriz, Touriga Franco

Altano Douro 79

Trincadeira, Aragonés

Paulo Laureano Clássico Vinho Regional 110

Verdejo

La Basca Verdejo 16
Tramoya Rueda Verdejo 29

Viognier

Les Perles Viognier Vin de Pays d'Oc 37